WE CAN TEACH
YOU TO PLAY
SOCCER

WE CAN TEACH YOU TO PLAY SOCCER

by *Bill Muse*
with Dan White

Photographs by James Whittier Parker

Diagrams and drawings by Steve Gussman

HAWTHORN BOOKS, INC.
Publishers/NEW YORK

Library of Congress Catalog Card Number: 75-20906

ISBN: 0-8015-6911-7

2 3 4 5 6 7 8 9 10

Contents

Preface

This book is written for boys and girls, because soccer is a game for *all* young athletes. Balance, timing, coordination, power—the attributes of soccer—can be developed easily by both girls and boys with proper work habits and drills. In its primitive form, soccer was considered too rough for girls, who adopted a similar, but simplified, version of the game, which did not allow physical contact. In modern times, a more complete understanding of the benefits of sports for everyone, regardless of sex, has encouraged more and more girls to develop their talents in a wide variety of sports, including soccer.

How do you learn to play soccer? First, and most important, one must learn the proper techniques—how to perform the basic skills of the game. Second, one must learn the game's strategies and style. For many years, American schoolchildren played what might be called "bicycle" soccer. They booted the ball from one end of the field to the other, back and forth, so fast that players almost needed bicycles to catch up with the flying ball. That's not the way the game is meant to be played.

Third, developing physical fitness is absolutely essential. But this is not really a problem if one already gets lots of exercise regularly. Soccer is a vigorous game, and the best players have at least one trait in common—endurance. They can run at different speeds for long periods of time without appearing to tire. Keep in mind that strength and endurance also are necessary for learning quickly and performing well.

This book describes and illustrates the correct techniques for learning how to play soccer and developing one's skills. It offers a range of practice drills, from the simple to the more advanced, from stationary exercises to game situations. Of course, a book can only do so much. Your success as an athlete depends on your willingness to constantly practice the skills described in this book.

Acknowledgments

I am indebted to many people, who have contributed their experiences and knowledge, which has greatly assisted me in the preparation of this book: Don Betterton, Dettmar Cramer, Dr. Joseph Machnik, Irv Schmid, Al Miller, and Walter Chyzowych; and the Fédération Internationale de Football Association and the United States Soccer Federation. I am grateful also to Messrs. Paul Gardner, Brian Glanville, and Allen Wade, whose books have provided me with both instruction and enjoyment. Many thanks, too, to Ms. Christine McKinley, who transmitted the copy into manuscript form.

WE CAN TEACH
YOU TO PLAY
SOCCER

Introduction

Soccer in the United States

Soccer, for Americans, is a game whose time has finally come. During the 1970s, soccer has become the fastest-growing sport in the United States. Ten years ago, only 25 percent of American colleges and universities had soccer programs. Today, the figure is over 50 percent. Since 1967, there have been two professional soccer leagues—the older American Soccer League (ASL, 1933) and the newer North American Soccer League (NASL, 1967). In 1975, one of the world's most famous players, Pelé of Brazil, joined the New York Cosmos (NASL), focusing worldwide attention on United States soccer. The growth and progress of professional leagues have motivated more young Americans to take up the game.

The collegiate and professional teams form the tip of a huge pyramid that includes a rapidly growing number of boys and girls at the elementary school level. More than 40,000 boys now play organized soccer in California, and 20,000 play in Washington state. During the past seven years Atlanta's Youth Soccer League has grown to 253 teams. In 1975, the premier Florida Youth Cup drew more than 60 clubs. Among the crowd at the first home game of Denver's professional soccer team in the 1975 season were more than 5,000 boys in their soccer uniforms.

As a game that includes most of the activities natural for youngsters—running, jumping, dodging, outwitting an opponent—soccer's appeal is increasing fast among girls. In 1967, there were no high school girls' teams registered with the United States Soccer Football Association, the governing body for soccer in this country. By 1974, 245 schools had programs. Of the 94 regional champion teams competing in the California State finals, 22 were girls' teams. The small town of Lawrenceville, New Jersey, had 5 peewee girls' teams in 1975. Internationally, in 1971 the first World Cup for women was played in Mexico City.

Soccer's Universal Appeal

Soccer has long been the most popular sport in the world. Today it is played in 140 nations by nearly 16 million athletes. An estimated 800 million people watched the televised final match for the 1970 World Cup, symbolic of the championship of the world, between Brazil and Italy. Soccer stadiums regularly accommodate crowds of over 100,000. Maracana Stadium in Brazil, a half-mile round, seats 200,000.

There are many reasons for the surge in popularity of soccer in the United States and for its traditional success throughout the world. Foremost is the nature of the game, with free-lance plays and swift, continuous action. The game seldom stops, because substitution is not allowed except for injury, and there is little coaching from the sidelines to slow the tempo. The combination of individual skills and team play produces a blend of artistry, drama, and excitement that has universal appeal for athlete and spectator alike.

The game is easy to understand. The purpose of play is immediately clear—to score a goal by propelling the ball into a net. The ball is always in view, so that the basic patterns of offense and defense are simple to follow.

Such simplicity, though a prized virtue, is deceptive—and that's another reason for the game's popularity—soccer has many different levels of skills. In its most elementary form, children kick a ball as they might kick a tin can along a street. At its highest plane, the best players control the ball as though it were tied by a string to their feet. They may know as many as twenty different techniques for kicking a ball, and they usually are adept with both feet.

Another reason for soccer's widespread appeal is that athletes don't have to be tall or big to play. Pelé is 5'8" and weighs 165 pounds. Physical contact is incidental to the game and is not a major tactic as in American football and rugby. A player may use his shoulder to contact an opponent who has the ball, but not violently or from the rear. Pure skills—instant and complete ball control, nimbleness, and endurance—and desire are what count.

Soccer is one of the few team sports in which an individual can develop his skills working by himself. He needs only a ball and a small area in which to practice—a wall, backyard, blacktop, or a corner of a field will do. He does not need a lot of expensive protective equipment. A jacket or shirt on the ground will serve as an opponent or as a goal.

History

The concept of football is ancient, although its actual origin is unknown. A primitive form of the game is mentioned in a Chinese military text of the third or fourth century B.C. Greek children knew a version of the game, and Roman legions spread a variety called *harpastum* throughout Europe and into Britain, where it developed through the centuries into a rough sport. In England village games often lasted several hours and involved hundreds of players. The goals were at opposite ends of the town, as distant as half a mile. These mob games were unruly and dangerous—kicking and tripping were accepted tactics—and there were many attempts to ban them. In 1314, Edward II of England declared that "hustling over large balls . . . [causes] . . . many evils," and forbade "on pain of imprisonment such games to be used in the future." In the sixteenth century Queen Elizabeth I commanded that "no foteballe play be used or suffered within the City of London." This attitude was not unlike President Theodore Roosevelt's feeling toward American football, which he threatened to outlaw for excessive roughness in the early 1900s. But football persisted. It was adopted by British public schools and universities, evolving through rule changes into three kinds of football: American, rugby, and soccer.

Britain exported soccer—or association football, as it is also known in other countries (the term "soccer" is a clipped adaptation of "association")—to the rest of the world. By the beginning of this century, international tournaments were being scheduled, professional leagues being developed and the Fédération Internationale de Football Association (FIFA), the governing body of association football, had been organized, with headquarters in Zurich, Switzerland. FIFA has 6 regional confederations: Europe, South America, Central and North America, Asia, Africa, and Australasia, each of which has wide control over discipline and competitions within its area. One of the aims of FIFA was to organize a world championship to be staged every four years between Olympic games. Regional competition for one of the final places (now 16 altogether) begins 2 years prior to the championships. The first tournament in 1930 attracted 13 countries and was won by Uruguay, indicating the rapid spread of soccer in Latin America. The last several World Cup competitions have drawn over 70 countries.

Soccer's popularity in the United States was limited at first to cities with large colonies of immigrants, such as New York, Boston, Philadelphia, and St. Louis. The American public at large seemed uninterested in soccer, perhaps because it was a foreign game that seemed slow and noncombative in comparison to American football. In 1913, the United States Soccer Federation was formed; college, secondary school, and professional teams began to organize, and gradually a total structure evolved, encompassing schoolboy to professional star, similar to systems in England and the rest of the world.

Rules

It has been said that the essence of soccer is its simplicity. This holds true for its rules, too, of which there are only 17. Basically, they have remained unchanged since 1925. Each of the 17 laws, as they are formally known, is listed in the appendix of this book. To provide a thumbnail sketch of how the game is played, the basic features are as follows: The field is 120 yards long by 75 yards wide, about as long as a football field with end zones, half again as wide. The women's field is 80–100 yards long and 40–60 yards wide.

Eleven players form a side; they are traditionally designated as goalkeeper, two fullbacks, three halfbacks, five forwards. The ball is an inflated rubber bladder encased in leather 27–28 inches round, 14–16 ounces in weight. Each team tries to advance the ball toward the opponent's goal by passing with the head or foot from one teammate to another, or by dribbling (dribbling is a series of taps, usually made with the instep or the side of the foot).

Only the goalkeeper is allowed to handle the ball—that is, to touch the ball with his hand or arm. The goalkeeper is restricted to a rectangular penalty area extending 18 yards into the field in front of the goal.

A game is 90 minutes long, divided into 45-minute halves. Women and schoolchildren often play shorter games, usually 30-minute halves. A single referee supervises the game and keeps time; he is assisted by two linesmen who patrol the sidelines (touchlines) and signal when the ball goes out of bounds.

When the ball travels over the touchlines, it is put back in play with a two-handed, over-the-head throw from outside the field.

There are 4 main categories of violations for which the offended team receives some measure of compensation:

1. *Direct free kick.* If a player intentionally commits a serious offense, such as holding, pushing, kicking, tripping, violently charging an opponent, or handling the ball, the guilty team surrenders the ball to an opponent who has the option to kick for a goal or pass to his teammates from the spot of the foul. "Direct" means the opponent can score from such a kick, although the ball usually needs to be within 30 yards of the goal before this is likely. If a player commits a serious foul within his own penalty area (around the goal his team is defending), the result is the award of a penalty kick to the other team.

2. *Penalty kick.* Except for the goalkeeper and the kicker, all players of both teams leave the penalty area. The ball is placed on a penalty spot 12 yards from the goal. The goalkeeper cannot move his feet until the ball is kicked. In top-level soccer, a penalty kick generally results in a goal, although the battle of nerves or the goalkeeper's extraordinary luck in anticipating the direction of the kick sometimes prevents this.

3. *Indirect free kick.* For less serious offenses, such as obstructing an opponent, ungentlemanly conduct, illegal substitution, and the goalkeeper carrying the ball more than 4 steps, the opponent has a free kick, but the ball must be touched by another player before a goal can be scored. An offsides penalty is punished in this way.

4. *Offside.* The purpose of this rule is to prevent attacking players from loitering around the goal to wait for long passes to score easy goals. When the ball is passed to an attacker, there must be at least two opposing players, one of them is usually the goalkeeper, nearer the goal than he. There are exceptions: A player cannot be offside if the ball is nearer the goal than he, or if the ball was last touched by an opponent, or if the attacker is standing in his own half of the field.

Strategies

The strategies of play have varied in the past 40 years. In the 1930s it was popular to pull back the center halfback to make him a third defensive back, leaving 4 forwards instead of 5. Italy introduced a system with a man roaming free behind 4 defenders to plug holes wherever they developed. This defensive approach was encouraged by early European tournaments, where the team with the greatest aggregate of goals was pronounced winner. To win, the chief tactic was to emphasize defense and stop other teams from scoring. After World War II, the center forward was stationed behind the attack in an effort to trick the opposing center halfback into leaving his defensive zone vulnerable to the inside forwards. In today's games, specialists such as wings, defensive backs, and center forwards, who play only a particular area of the field, have given way to all-around players, and to the concept of total attack and defense. The forwards become the initial line of defense whenever possession of the ball is lost. The midfielders link attack to defense and must play both ends of the field. The goalkeeper and defenders are the instigators of the quick counterattack. The emphasis for players is on total development of every facet of the game.

1
Juggling

Definition

A clever juggler at a circus can keep several balls in the air for a long time. He has developed excellent hand-eye coordination as the result of many hours of practice. When a soccer player juggles, he taps a single ball into the air over and over again without letting it fall to the ground. Some European players can juggle a soccer ball 2 to 3 hours, without letting the ball hit the ground. A soccer juggler not only uses his feet but also his head and thighs to keep the ball in the air.

The purpose of juggling is to learn to control the ball with the same parts of the body—feet, thighs, and head—that are used to receive and control passes. Juggling alone will not make a proficient soccer player, but it will help you develop confidence, balance, and speed with the ball.

Confidence comes from knowing you can take a pass at 60 miles per hour out of the air and settle it, or that you can gather a 65-yard kick from the goalkeeper and relay it with pace and accuracy to a teammate.

Juggling heightens your sense of touch and balance. You become familiar with every bounce and roll of the ball. Adeptness at juggling leads to quickness with the ball. You must be able to knock down the ball in one fluid motion with your body and move it immediately. If you have to pause to regain your balance after you stop the ball, you lose time and you decrease the space between you and the opponent.

The main points of learning how to juggle are: form a flat plane with each part of the body that touches the ball so the ball rebounds vertically; soften the rebound to maintain control; and establish a rhythm to your taps that will be helpful in achieving control.

Foot Juggling

When juggling with the feet, concentrate first on obtaining a straight up and down rebound of the ball. Bend the knee and lock your ankle with the instep parallel to the ground, just as you would in the instep pass. Now, however, the laces point straight up. The ball should travel

directly upward off the laces of your shoe. Aim for the center of the underside of the ball. If you hit it off center, it will spin away at an angle.

To begin foot juggling, take the ball with your hands and drop it. As the ball falls, kick it gently back to your hands. Drop the ball again and repeat, but this time play the ball twice before returning it to your hands. Build your rebounds one at a time, trying to beat your previous record. As you become more confident, use your other foot, and then alternate feet, by playing it once with the right, then left, right, etc. Moderate the force of each tap and establish a rhythm.

Thigh

To juggle using your thigh, raise your leg and flex your knee so that your thigh is parallel to the ground. The top of the thigh is flat and provides a broad surface for juggling. Drop the ball onto this movable landing pad. Be sure to lift your thigh to meet the ball so it will rebound vertically. Control the bounce—it should rise about chest high. If the ball flies away from you, your thigh isn't level enough; or else you're hitting the ball too near your knee.

As soon as you're accustomed to these movements, use your feet to tap the ball onto your thigh. Increase your record of consecutive taps, as you did in foot juggling. How soon can you do 50–100 taps? Switch and alternate thighs.

Head

In juggling with the head, the middle forehead contacts the ball. Bend your head backward and point your forehead straight up. Keep a fairly stiff neck and your eyes wide open. As you play the ball vertically with your head, push up from your knees. Although you contact the ball with only one small area, the whole body is involved in control of the juggle. Make the ball bounce vertically from your forehead. A good height is about 12–14 inches.

Practice head juggling by throwing the ball straight up with the hands, about 12 inches in front of you, no more than 2 feet above your head. Build from 1 touch, to 2 touches, 3 touches, etc.

Lifting the Ball

Now is the time to stop using your hands in your juggling, because a field player never uses his hands or arms. There are a number of ways to lift the ball into play. One easy method is to roll the ball backwards with the sole of the foot on to your instep, quickly scoop it upward with your instep, and then begin juggling. Another is to pinch the ball between your feet and jump, lifting the ball up high enough so it can be hit easily with the foot or thigh. Once you know these methods, try to scoop the ball with the instep from the ground into the air in one sweeping motion.

To pick up a ball at rest between the feet, pinch the toes tightly together. The ball will pop up high enough for you to tap it with one foot and begin juggling.

To lift the ball with a "rainbow," place one foot in front of a still ball with the heel resting against the ball. The other foot is behind the ball, with half the instep covering the ball. Now start forward by lifting the back foot first. This movement will cause the ball to roll slightly up onto the heel of the front foot. Now kick it up and over the back of your head to your front.

Juggling on the Move

After you gain confidence juggling with each of the 3 body parts while standing still, learn to perform on the move. Start by walking, and then progress to a trotting pace. It is entirely different and much more difficult to control the ball while moving. Keep at it, because constant practice will give you the confidence to perform these skills under match conditions.

Juggling in Sequence

Move next to overall juggling—the use of thighs, head, and feet, in sequence, tapping the ball from one body part to another. Build toward this goal by simply beginning as you did previously. Start at the feet. Juggle the ball twice with the feet. On the second touch, add a little extra lift, so the ball can be played easily with the thighs. In the same way, move the ball from either the feet or the thighs to the head. Then reverse the process by starting with the head, proceeding to the thighs, and ending with the feet. Mix up the sequence. Keep the ball rebounding as long as possible without touching the ball more than twice in succession with any one body part. Change the heights of the rebounds and then begin moving around while you juggle.

Remember that juggling helps you learn to feel at ease with the ball. But don't become so addicted to juggling that you neglect other fundamental skills. You want to become a good soccer player, not a circus performer.

2
Passing

Definition

Although solo runs and dribbles are spectacular, passing is the most important feature of soccer. Boys and girls who have played games like lacrosse and field hockey will already understand the need for good passing. Seventy-five to 80 percent of all ball releases in a match are passes. To win games, a team must advance the ball consistently and keep possession of it longer than its opponents. This is best achieved by passing the ball to a teammate who is in a more advantageous position than you—either free of an opponent or about to become free. In a split second, you must compute the distance, speed, direction, and height of your pass. It is not enough to merely boot the ball toward a teammate. The pass must be tempered so the receiver can stop, control, and redirect it. Pass the ball to the player or to a space where he can run to receive the ball free of interference by an opponent.

Push Pass

The most basic pass in soccer, the push pass, is performed with the inside of the foot. The inside of the foot is preferred because it provides accuracy and a speedy release. Another advantage of this pass is that you can combine in one easy motion the inside-of-the-foot trap with a push pass. Kicking this way is not a usual skill for American boys and girls, who tend to kick with their toes as in a football place kick. Compared to the inside of the foot, which is a long straight surface, the toe is small and pointed. It's the same as hitting a golf ball on the end of a putter instead of the side. There's no comparison in accuracy.

To execute the push pass, place the nonkicking foot beside the ball, toe aimed at the target. Turn your kicking foot outward so the anklebone faces straight ahead and the foot forms a right angle to the ball. The heels of both feet should almost meet. Bend the kicking knee

slightly. Lift the lower leg from the knee, not the hip; pull your toe up as if trying to touch the shin, and strike the ball dead center just in front of the anklebone. At contact, the knee is over the ball. If the knee is too far behind the ball, the foot will tend to swing upward; if too far in front, the foot will squeeze the ball into the ground. The motion of the lower leg should be like the swing of a pendulum. Follow through, pointing the anklebone up and toward the direction of the pass. To keep the ball low, aim through the upper half of the ball or just above it. If you hit below the center line, you probably will lift the ball. Follow-through is important; a good push pass will travel along the ground in the direction you are facing, so do not stop your kick at the point of contact nor too abruptly in front of you.

A frequent mistake in the early stages of learning this pass is an inclination for the player to lean back as he pushes the ball. This will cause the ball to rise and will reduce its velocity. It may mean, too, that the player swings across rather than through the ball.

Instep Pass

The instep pass is for kicking forcefully and accurately over long distances. Approach the ball from a slight angle rather than straight on. The nonkicking foot points toward the target, as in the push pass. Hit the ball with the laces of your kicking shoe, toes curled under to make your instep an extension of the leg. The kicking foot does not turn outward as with the push pass, but locks straight downward. The snap of your lower leg must be vigorous. Strike the ball with a stiff ankle, firmly and fully on the laces.

The speed of the kicking foot as it thumps the ball determines the amount of power. A common error in learning this kick is to swing a lazy leg from the hip and not whip the lower leg through the ball.

When this happens, more often than not you will loosen your ankle, widen the arc of your swing, and kick up a divot of grass. The instep pass takes lots of practice, but you gain a double skill—for most of your shots on goal are made with the instep kick. Accuracy, therefore, is essential.

By the way, if you have a hard time curling your toes underneath to stretch your instep, lie on your stomach, extend your toes as far as they go, and try to touch all of your laces to the ground with flutter kicks, like a swimmer. After a few weeks, the fronts of your feet will be stretched sufficiently to allow you to form a straight line from knee to toe when you execute the instep pass.

Flick Pass

The outside of the foot, or flick pass, is done essentially the same way as the instep kick. One foot is stationary beside the ball but not pointed at the target, since the ball is to be struck this time with the outside of the kicking foot. Swing the kicking foot away from the midline of the body. The knee leads, followed by the ankle, then the rest of the foot, each straightening in quick succession. Since you are

striking the ball with the outside of your foot, the knee does not pass over the ball as it would in the instep kick. For absolute accuracy, the player must watch his foot strike through the ball. This pass is especially deceptive because you can run in one direction and deliver the ball to the right or left at any angle without crossing one foot in front of the other.

Chipping

In golf, a short drive that flies high in the air and lands softly on the green is a chip shot. In soccer, chipping describes how you kick the ball with backspin in a high arc to make it land gently. Chipping is used in free kicks and corners, as well as in regular play. Most chipped shots occur with the ball at rest.

Approach the ball from an angle. The nonkicking foot aligns 2 feet to the side, even with the ball. The last step by the supporting leg should be long enough to permit the kicking leg to swing at an angle to

the direction the pass will travel. Lean your body backwards so that the kicking leg is fully extended at impact. Kick the bottom of the ball to impart back spin but, contrary to other passes, do not follow through. The chopped swing helps reverse the spin of the ball, and the backspin helps the ball grip the turf when it lands.

If you have trouble getting height on the ball you might be aiming too high on the ball. Or you may be lifting your head, which causes a slight straightening of the body and raises your kicking foot. Another mistake is to throw your weight down instead of through the ball, causing you to kick too far under it and lose distance and control.

Swerving

Swerving the ball is a more advanced skill, not to be tried until novice players have mastered the basic passes. This pass can be used over long distances to bend the ball around defenders and make it spin in the direction a teammate is running. There are times, too, especially on corner kicks or shots on goal, when kicking a ball to make it curve in flight and then bounce in the opposite direction is useful in trying to fool a goalkeeper.

Approach the ball on more of a straight line than you would on the instep kick. Contact is made with the instep, but spin is imparted to the

ball by hitting it off-center. The ball swerves in the direction of the spin; if you strike it just left of center, the ball will curve from left to right; right of center, the ball travels from right to left. As you can imagine, achieving accuracy takes lots of hard practice and time that you can't spare until you have mastered the other, more immediately valuable passes.

Throw-In

Different from every other type of pass is the throw-in from out of bounds. The rule states that the ball must be thrown with both hands in one continuous motion from the back of the head to the front without either foot leaving the ground or entering the field of play. One method is to take the ball behind the head, step forward with one leg so that your legs are split apart, and throw.

A second method is a lateral approach, with both feet square and pointed straight ahead.

In both cases, arch the back and whip the ball. Use legs, back, and arms to generate power. A good throw-in is just as important as a field pass in maintaining possession or in attacking the defense. A long throw-in in the offensive sector automatically becomes as dangerous as a corner kick, because the ball is served up right in front of the goal.

A team that has one player who is very good at lengthy, accurate throws should make him its throw-in specialist. By repetition of correct technique, you can increase the distance of your throws and benefit your team greatly.

Common Mistakes

The most glaring faults of passing are: passing with the toe; lifting the head; swinging across the ball (push pass) rather than through it; not swinging the lower leg vigorously on the instep kick; kicking the ball off-center; trying to kick too hard; and not following through in the prescribed manner.

Drills

You can practice most passes by yourself. Find a wall and pass the ball against it. First, stop each return. Then do continuous 2-touch passing, steadying the ball only for an instant before you return it. Follow that by hitting the ball back without stopping it at all. Use the instep, the inside and outside of both feet. Run parallel to the wall, striking the ball right and left with the inside and outside of the feet.

If you have a partner, you can repeat the same drills and then play some passing games. Each of you has a ball. Your partner tries to hit your stationary ball with his, using 1 of 3 passes. You in turn, aim at his ball when it comes to rest. You can play this all over the field. For variety, rule that the ball cannot be stopped before each pass. For each hit of the opponent's ball, you receive one goal. Concentrate on one type of pass at a time.

You can also play soccer-golf, using cones or sticks to design a miniature golf course. Pass the ball to a particular stick. How many passes does it take to hit the stick? Lowest number wins. Use all the different passes.

Another contest involves more players—1 on 2, 4 on 4. Set up 2 small goals—cones, shirts, balls, whatever. No goalkeepers. Each player may move the ball only with a designated part of the foot. If anyone uses a different portion of the foot, it's a foul and the ball goes to the other team.

To practice chipping, return to the wall. Begin with a stationary ball and stop it on the rebound every time before you chip it again. Next, chip a moving ball. Have a friend stand 25–30 yards away to receive passes from you.

From a distance of about 30 yards, kick towards the goal and attempt to chip the ball over the crossbar. How close can you come to the goal and still chip the ball over?

Kick from the edge of the penalty area toward the middle of the field so the ball lands softly in the center circle without rolling out.

Accuracy is your first concern in practicing the throw-in. To perfect your form, start by throwing from a kneeling position. Progress to your feet, and work on your upper body movement to develop power. Have throw-in contests for distance and accuracy. Your next concern must be quickness. The key to all throw-ins is to get the ball in play quickly before the other team can regroup its defense. When you are ready for a partner, there are different situations that can be practiced quite easily to help you develop a sense of timing and anticipation of each other's movements.

The person receiving the throw-in indicates to the thrower through simple hand signals where he will run to receive the throw-in. In most cases, the receiver will be marked from behind. The receiver hides his hand in front of his chest, points the direction he'll go, pretends he'll go the opposite way, then darts open for the ball. If he wants the ball thrown at his feet, he points to his feet; high, to his head; and so forth.

After you have developed a good throw-in routine with your partner, enlist a third person to be a defender and practice 2 against 1.

3
Trapping

Definition

Trapping refers to an assortment of techniques with which we receive an incoming ball and control it as quickly as possible. If your body is stiff and unyielding, the ball will bounce away as if you were a wall, and you will spend your time chasing the ball all over the field. Careful attention to correct procedure for trapping and constant practice of juggling to increase overall body feel for the ball will teach you how to subdue a hard pass and gain complete, immediate control with the foot, chest, thigh, and head—the main parts used for trapping.

Principles of Trapping

There are three things to consider when you trap a ball: First, always advance to meet the ball. Never wait for the ball to come to you, and never let the ball bounce first if it can be helped. A bounce increases

the chance of error and reduces the time and space you have available
to prepare the ball for the next play. If you are going to trap on the
run, slow down to steady your body and gain balance as you receive
the ball. Do not attempt to run full throttle before the ball is settled.

Second, always present a flat surface of your body to land the ball.
The body surface should be perpendicular to the flight of the ball.

Third, and most important, always give with the ball to absorb its
momentum. As you receive the ball, relax the stopping surface to take
the speed off the ball, so it drops gently at your feet and can be
dribbled or passed right away.

Foot

Of the four parts of the body used to land the ball, the foot is the most widely employed. To take a ball out of flight, use the topside of your foot, the laces. Extend the foot with the knee bent and the lower leg lifted in advance of the knee so that the laces are perpendicular to the path of the ball and aimed at its center. Just before impact, withdraw the foot to reduce the speed of the ball in the same way you might use your bare hand to cushion the force of a baseball.

Use the sole of your foot to stop a pass rolling along the field. Stretch your leg forward, with the knee slightly bent, and the heel about 6 inches off the ground, toe inclined upward. Bend your foot

down at impact so the sole contacts the upper half of the ball. Do not step on the ball. Again, relax your foot so the ball doesn't rebound away.

The inside and outside of the foot can also be tilted to trap passes. To do the inside of the foot, rotate the ankle outward as in the push pass. Let your foot and lower leg give with the ball slightly so there is no rebound. This is the primary way to receive passes on the ground as well as balls up to 3 feet off the ground.

To trap with the outside of the foot, cross the trapping leg in front of the supporting leg and fix the ball between the outside of the foot and the ground. Because proper balance is harder to maintain and it is more difficult to cushion the ball with the outside of the foot, this trap is most often preferred when it is necessary to move speedily away from an opponent as the ball is received.

Chest

In the chest trap for boys, the target is the chest bone. Inflate your lungs slightly and move your shoulders forward to flatten your chest. If the pass is high and descending sharply, rock back (same as in the throw-in) and show the ball your chest. When the ball touches, withdraw and straighten your upper body and bring the ball down to your feet. A common error is to bend backward too soon, so that when the ball arrives the chest cannot give further and the ball bounces away.

Girls employ a different technique for the chest trap. You are permitted to tuck the fists under the chin, elbows together, and play the ball off the forearms. The rules do not, however, allow you to catch the ball with the arms. You must maneuver the ball away from the body, moderating the force of the rebound by relaxing the arms at impact.

Thigh

If it is necessary to stop the ball with your thigh, bend the knee of the trapping leg to form a flat area on the thigh. The amount the knee bends is dictated by the angle of the ball's approach. The steeper the arc of the ball, the higher the knee must be raised to maintain a 90-degree relationship with the ball. Take the ball on the fleshy part of the upper thigh. As the ball begins to make contact, start to withdraw the thigh to cushion the ball and guide it to rest at your feet.

Head

The head is a more difficult instrument for trapping. Use the forehead. Lock the ball into your forehead, then give, just like a big spring, on the recoil, by bending your knees, and drawing in the neck and head to cushion the impact. If the ball is too high and you are forced to jump, time your leap just a split second early so that you contact the ball just as you have started to descend. The downward motion of the body acts as the cushion on the ball.

Common Errors

The two most common mistakes in trapping are failure to relax on contact with the ball and poor balance as the body sets itself for the trap.

Drills

To practice your trapping skills by yourself, you can use two methods. The first is to throw the ball up and bring it to rest at your feet by using the head, chest, thighs, and feet. The problem here is that you get basically only one angle of flight. A better way, which incorporates all angles, is to throw or kick the ball at different heights against a wall. Wait for the rebound, decide which part of the body you wish to use, and then, after settling the ball, move quickly to the right or left to free yourself from an imaginary defender.

After you gain confidence in trapping balls at different angles with both feet, thighs, head, and chest, and in moving off quickly, ask a friend to toss a ball to you from about 10–15 yards away in different directions. The next step is to have him rush toward you to place pressure on you just after he releases the ball. After you have trapped it, either get out of trouble by running away from the defender, or settle the ball and bypass the defender with a dribble. This will give you confidence under match conditions. Work to make the trap and the first move of the dribble one continuous movement. Begin with individual practice and move on to sprinting under challenge from the opponents. This is the ultimate purpose of trapping—bringing the ball under control while under pressure.

4
Heading

Definition

Soccer is the only major ball sport in the world in which players deliberately use their heads to strike the ball. Because the head is hard, it can be used like a fist to hit the ball with enormous power at the goal, or it can be used less forcefully to pass to a teammate or to gently guide the ball to the ground for immediate play.

Does It Hurt?

Heading a ball correctly does not hurt. Prove it to yourself. Hold a ball in front of you and toss it at your forehead. Keep your eyes open and strike the ball with your forehead. Try to watch the ball land on the center of your forehead—if you close your eyes, you may catch the ball on your nose or on the crown of your skull. If you wear glasses, follow the same technique, but be doubly certain to hit the ball with the forehead. With or without glasses, you will be inclined to blink just as the ball hits your forehead, but this involuntary action lasts only a fraction of a second. Repeat this exercise several times, throwing harder and harder until you're convinced there's no pain involved.

Form

All heading is done using essentially the same form. Face the ball, try to get directly under it, and hit it with the center, flat area of the forehead (eyes open!) As you prepare to hit the ball, arch your back, pull in your chin, and tense the muscles of your neck. Just prior to impact, thrust your head through the ball as if someone had suddenly poked you in the stomach. This vigorous push of the head gives an explosive power to the ball.

It's essential that you attack the ball with your head and not allow it to land on your head. If you were trapping the ball, you'd pull in your head and neck like a turtle, but since you're propelling the ball to a distant spot, you must apply force—in different degrees, depending on the situation.

Changing Direction

You can change the direction of the ball by turning your forehead and hitting through the ball in the direction it is to travel. Contact is still made with the flat part of the forehead. Beginners often nod the ball with the side of their head rather than twisting the upper body and forehead around to face the ball.

Jump Heading

Many times in a game a player must jump high to head a ball. To gain maximum height, leap off one foot and pull your arms forward and up over your head like a diver on a springboard. Time your jump so that

you strike the ball while at maximum height. You will appear to hover in mid-air, your back arched like a cheerleader's. Just before contact, straighten your back and strike the ball with the forehead. The secret of meeting the ball squarely is timing. Inexperienced players usually jump too late and have no time to bend the back and spring forward. The result is a limp body that provides no direction and little impetus to the headed ball.

Dive Heading

Although a player should always remain balanced on his feet, there are some occasions when the ball can be reached only by diving for it.

A diving header is one way to reach low hard balls out of range of your legs, but it is a secondary technique suitable for more advanced players. The most difficult and important part of diving to head a ball is the landing. As you stretch out in mid-air, get both hands and arms down quickly. They are your shock absorbers, so they must strike the ground before the body to take up most of the impact. Otherwise, the basic principles are the same. Strike the ball with the forehead, shooting the head forward just before impact. The body is parallel to the ground when the ball is hit, and the hands have started to move down to cushion the fall.

Common Mistakes

Common mistakes in heading are: not hitting the ball with the front of the forehead; closing the eyes before contact; and jumping too late to head high balls.

Drills

Practice the basic form and movement of heading by kneeling and having someone toss a ball for you to head. Progress to a standing

position, feet parallel to each other. Head the ball firmly back to your friend's hands, then to the feet, and then up over the head.

Practice jump heading with a partner who stands and holds a ball aloft with two hands. You jump and hit your head against the held ball to practice arching the back and forcefully springing the body and head forward. Next, have your partner throw high passes that you jump to.

HEADING

To learn to head the ball from a diving position, kneel and fall forward, dropping the arms as if you were going to do push-ups. Move next to a squatting position. When you've become familiar with the landing routine, repeat the different positions, this time with a ball in play.

5
Dribbling

Dribbling

When you dribble, you advance the ball with soft rapid touches of the foot. That is how you keep possession of the ball and try to take it past one or more opponents. The virtuosity of soccer skills is most apparent in dribbling. The old master dribblers like Sir Stanley Matthews of England, Alfredo di Stefano of Spain, and Ferenc Puskas of Hungary, could beat their defenders at will, manipulating their feet the way a juggler or magician uses his hands. Matthews would bring the ball squarely to the defender. He would lean so far in one direction that it would seem obvious that he had to go that way, but his balance was so perfect that he would tap the ball the other way, accelerate, and dart past the groping defender, who often resorted illegally to grabbing Matthews's shirt.

In recent years, dribbling has been discouraged for the sake of the passing game, but if dribbling is properly understood and employed it adds immensely to a player's overall effectiveness. The value of beating opponents while running with the ball under close control should never be underestimated. Penetrating the inner defense by dribbling is one of the keystones of attack. When there is one defender to beat for a shot on goal and no one to pass to, you must beat your opponent by dribbling.

But, on the contrary, dribbling for showmanship is self-defeating. A player who is unwilling to part with the ball disrupts a team's attack and its rhythm of play. If you dribble too long, or overdribble, without passing the ball, you become a one-man team, much to the dissatisfaction of your teammates.

When to Dribble

There are 3 strategic times for dribbling: first, when you penetrate the inner defense; second, when your teammates are checked and there is no one to pass to; and third, when you want to keep possession of the ball by shielding it from a defender.

How to Dribble

The 3 major points of dribbling are: (1) keeping the ball within playing distance; (2) maintaining balance to be able to move in any direction; and (3) using certain feints to draw the opponent off balance and run by him.

The force applied to the ball must be firm, but not too hard or too delicate. If it's too strong, the ball rolls beyond the area of tight control; if it's not firm, the ball lags at your feet, slows you down, and can trip you. Running at full speed, you can lay the ball further ahead, since you obviously can reach the ball more quickly.

In certain instances, it is advantageous to dribble with speed. Push the ball ahead some distance, but near enough that you can recover it before a defender interferes. When you have a wide open field or rush upfield to initiate a counterattack, you employ speed dribbling. A front runner enroute to the goal dribbles in full stride. It is best, however, for young athletes learning to dribble, to keep the ball close to their feet, to develop control first and speed later.

Split Vision

A skilled dribbler splits his vision between the ball and the field of play or the opponent whom he is trying to dodge and dribbles without focusing attention on the ball. To watch only the ball makes it impossible to see what other players nearby are doing. Young players must develop a sense of where the ball is.

Basic Feints

Tightly controlled dribbling is necessary for beating an opponent in a confined area. There are several techniques to draw an opponent off balance so you can run by him. A few expertly done feints are preferable to a bag full of halfway effective tricks.

A change of pace and direction are the most basic dodges. A good dribbler should approach his opponent slowly to get him to relax or let up his concentration. At the right time, change your pace from slow to quick—that's easier than going from quick to quicker. Vary the speed

of your approach and leave something in reserve so you can accelerate at the right time. The ability to dart ahead, often from standstill, in 5–10 yards stretches is vital to effective dribbling.

One way to suddenly change direction is to play the ball back with the inside foot (either foot) in the direction opposite to which you are running. If you run to your right, tap the ball with the right foot back to the left, shift your body, and be off before the defender can recover and reverse his direction. This is a nice maneuver against an adversary who charges directly at you. Simply anchor the left foot, lean right, and cut the ball back to the left, across the defender's path. Be

patient—wait for the moment when your opponent has irreversably committed himself in one direction.

Another tactic is to hit the ball back with the outside of the foot. Run to the left dribbling with the right foot. Your left leg is the pivot leg. Swing the lower leg of your kicking foot in front of the pivot leg and nudge the ball with the outer surface, from the left back to the right. Follow through in the new direction of the ball. Try to further deceive the opponent by leaning your upper body slightly in the direction opposite where you intend the ball to go.

If you have excellent speed and some time and space in which to

operate, push the ball by your opponent once he has drawn close, and sprint around him as he turns.

A stepover is a smart feint, but more for experienced players. As you move the ball toward an opponent, approach it with the right leg as if you are going to kick it. Instead, step over the ball so that you cross in front of your left leg, continue forward, and hit the ball with the inside of your left foot to the defender's right. Pivot on your right foot and pursue the ball. (See photo sequence on pages 62 and 63.)

The sole-of-the-foot roll is a maneuver best done with a ball at rest. Stop the ball momentarily, draw it in with the sole of your foot, then push it by your opponent. Do not place any weight on the ball, or you may turn your ankle or fall. (See illustrations on pages 64 and 65.)

The fake step-on can be executed at full speed or in resting position. Stop the ball and prepare to kick it, but hold it instead with the sole of the foot on top of the ball, then play it according to the reaction of your opponent.

Shielding

Shielding the ball means placing your body between the opponent and the ball while keeping it within playing distance. It may not seem to be dribbling, but it is. It's another device to maintain possession of the ball and also to bide time until teammates can move into open areas for a pass. If the defender is directly behind you, use your body to obstruct him—rump out, knees bent—as he goes after the ball.

Always keep your body between him and the ball, and watch him out of the corner of your eye so that you can position yourself as he moves about. You cannot block the opponent from the ball if neither of you are within playing distance of the ball. That would be considered obstruction by the referee.

Common Mistakes

The most frequent mistakes in dribbling are: pushing the ball too far ahead; dribbling without looking up; and not changing pace or direction.

Drills

Use a cone or chair as an unmoving defender and learn to beat it easily. Progress next to a moving defender and eventually to a goal (always try to have a goalkeeper when you shoot at the goal). Practice all the techniques by yourself and work up to real competition.

A good basic exercise is to simply push the ball along the ground in a straight line 15–20 yards, playing the ball with every other stride or every swing of the right or left leg. The better you get, the faster you should run. Then try variable speed running, stopping and starting, and sudden changes of direction.

An excellent all-around drill is for you and a friend to oppose each other in a ten-yard square or a small circle. Each takes a turn at dribbling in this confined space at constantly different speeds and directions, using your entire repertoire of moves. The person without the ball is the tackler. As a real test of skill, the dribbler can compete against two tacklers in the same limited space.

A different drill requires a group of players to stand in a small area while several more sit, hands touching the ground, stomachs upward, in a crab position. The upright players dribble in and around the "crabs," who remain down but can move around and tackle the ball. If they succeed in kicking the ball out of the circle three times, they exchange positions.

To improve your speed dribbling, have someone chase you toward the goal. Get to the goal and shoot as quickly as possible. Concentrate on speed, control, and scoring.

6
Shooting

Shooting

Scoring goals is the object of soccer. Mastery of all the other skills will mean little if a team cannot score. Since the number of goals in an average game is low, the instance of a forward kicking a ball into the net or leaping off the ground to head a goal is one of the most dramatic in all sports.

Accuracy and Power

To begin with, you must be able to kick accurately into any spot of the goal, an area that measures 8 by 24 feet. Speed of the shot is naturally important, but accuracy is what separates shooters from scorers.

Where to Shoot

Never push the ball randomly toward the goal. Aim for a spot such as the back corner of the net, on each side of the goal. These two corners

are good targets because they are usually beyond the range of the goalkeeper and enough inside the front posts to allow your shot to be off-target a little and still go into the goal.

Shots on the far post, or away from the goalkeeper, are also more difficult to stop than balls straight on. It is harder for the goalkeeper to reach such shots, and the motion of the ball away from him makes it more awkward to hold onto.

You must decide whether to shoot high or low. Shots along the ground cause goalkeepers the severest problems. They are susceptible to deflection, which makes the goalkeeper's job more difficult. It is easier for the goalkeeper to plot the flight of a ball in the air.

Side of the Foot

When you are within 10 yards of the goal, it may be more advantageous for you to pass the ball into the net with the side of your foot rather than try to blast it. A push pass employing all of the principles mentioned earlier in this book is the fastest and surest way to place the ball, especially when you have just dribbled by a defender and must shoot double quick.

Instep

For more power, kick with the instep, a slower, but much more vigorous and compact swing than the push pass. It is a common misconception that you have to be large to shoot with power. A smaller athlete using proper form can propel the ball with more zip than a much bigger player. The reason is, he concentrates his weight and power at precisely the moment he strikes the ball. The force of his kicking motion is so strong that on his followthrough he lands a yard or two ahead of where the ball was kicked from.

Here are the mechanics of shooting with the instep: Kick the ball with the full instep. Curl your toes under so that your foot is like a fist inside your shoe, and lock your ankle. Aim at the middle or upper part of the ball to keep it low. A ball kicked below its center line may rise over the top of the goal, resulting in loss of possession for the attackers. The nonkicking foot is placed alongside the ball. If it's behind the ball, the shot will rise over the goal. If the ball is rolling away as you prepare to shoot, place the supporting foot just in front of it to compensate for ball movement while your leg is swinging. Bend your leg so that the knee is directly over the ball at impact, and whip your lower leg and foot through the ball. Follow through with the foot and keep your head down. The time to sight your target is just before you shoot, not as you kick. If you jerk your head up to see where the ball

has gone, your leg will pull up and retard the accuracy of your kick. Lifting the head is a frequent mistake. Another is the tendency to overkill or kick too hard. Correct form will gain you all the power needed.

Volley

You don't always have as much time and room as you'd like to get off a shot. Many shots taken in a game come off bouncing or inflight balls. Shooting a ball that is already in the air is known as volley kicking. It's a good way to convert crossing kicks in front of the goal into scores.

For highest accuracy, a ball in flight should be kicked with the side of the foot in the same manner as the inside-of-the-foot pass—except, of course, the ball is off the ground. As the ball approaches, kick through the ball just above the center, to keep it low. If the incoming

ball is high and you want to kick for power, the technique is different. As you prepare to kick, point the supporting foot toward the target, lean away from the ball as if you were going to extend your body parallel to the ground, balancing on one leg. From this position, drive the lower leg through the ball, contacting it with the full instep.

Half Volley

A half volley is a ball kicked immediately after it bounces off the ground—on the short hop. The technique is the same as in kicking with the instep—sideways leg movement, propelling the lower leg through the upper part of the ball.

Swerve

You may have to curve your shot at the goalkeeper—not only to try to deceive him, but to get the ball around a wall of players who have aligned themselves in front of the goal. This situation arises most frequently on direct and indirect kicks near the goal area. In 1966 World Cup play, Brazil's Pelé was awarded a penalty kick against

Bulgaria just outside the penalty area. Four Bulgarians locked arms in front of the goal to form a wall, but Pelé hooked the ball around them into the net.

To review how to make the ball swerve, see Chapter 2 on passing. By contacting the ball in such a manner you lose some control over accuracy. That's why new players should first master the fundamental kicks and always depend on them as their primary weapons.

Heading

The front area of the goal often becomes congested, especially on corner kicks when defense and offense alike crowd into the area, jockeying for good position. In such a crowd, there is little time, if any, to settle the ball, and almost no space free of an opponent. A scorer who can jump and head an approaching ball into the net has a clear advantage over one who depends solely on kicking the ball. In heading to score, most of the time you will have to change the direction of the ball. Jump off one foot to gain as much height as possible. As you leap, pivot your body so you are facing the goal, and hammer the ball a little high of center with the front of the forehead. Aim for the goal line on the uncovered section of goal. This causes you to head the ball down. The most common mistake is to not turn the forehead but to use instead the side of the head. The result is a spinner that either falls limply to the ground or flies over the crossbar.

Drills

To develop power, the most important factor is the transfer of body weight through the ball. To practice this important principle, take the ball in your hands and run toward the goal. When you reach the edge of the 6-yard box, punt the ball on the run into the back of the net. The knee should be over the ball, upper body forward, and head down. If your form is incorrect, the ball will travel over the top of the goal. The second step is to drop-kick the ball into the net on the short half volley. Next, dribble forward and strike the ball from the ground as it rolls away.

After you learn to shoot with consistent power, work to develop accuracy. Start with still balls and concentrate on shooting with good form from 20 yards. Aim for high corners, low corners, posts, and crossbars. Hit moving balls, rolling them in front of you. Then, dribble, using feints and fakes. Practice trapping passes with your back to the goal, then turn and shoot. The next progression would be to shoot at the goal while a goalkeeper guards it.

There are many times in a game when you must shoot while moving across the penalty area parallel to the goal line. Plant your nonkicking foot ahead of the ball far enough to allow for the roll of the ball away from you. The kicking leg must be swung out and away somewhat to allow for the ball's movement. Weight transfer is a bit more difficult, because you must now turn your body away from the direction in which you are running and kick toward the goal. All other fundamentals are identical. Practice this skill by dribbling and rolling the ball across the edge of the penalty area, shooting on the move at top speed. Do this with a goalkeeper and against a defender.

To practice in the penalty area where time is precious, and instant and complete ball control essential, start by juggling about 10 times and then shoot the ball into the goal. Next, have a friend serve balls to you at many different angles and heights. Take the ball out of the air, settle it on the ground and score. Do this against a defender and with a goalkeeper.

If a goalkeeper is unavailable, or you are practicing alone, a wall or kickboard is an excellent teaching prop. You can shoot at will, playing rebounds or still balls without having to chase the ball after every shot—unless of course you miss the goal!

7
Tackling

Definition

Tackling means challenging an opponent who is in possession of the ball to steal or block it. Because tackling of a different sort is fundamental to American football, its purpose in soccer can be easily misunderstood. The most important thing to remember is that it is far more beneficial if you learn and condition yourself to first play correct defense; then the number of times you will have to tackle will be kept to a minimum.

The skill of tackling is necessary for all positions, since all players have defensive responsibilities. There are different techniques, some of which are more likely to be used at different positions than others. A halfback more often employs a front block tackle, because attackers approach him head on. Forwards might rely more on side blocks, since their major defensive role usually involves chasing the ball. The sliding tackle, usually a last-ditch, high-risk maneuver, is used by fullbacks along the touchlines to poke the ball out of bounds, or when an attacker has broken away and the defender must stop him at all costs.

Principles

There are several guiding principles to effective tackling. The first is to force your man to an area where there is the least possible risk to the goal if your tackle fails. Ideally, you should try to tackle in a confined space—when you have your opponent hemmed in against the touchline, for instance. Another consideration is defensive backup. Are you covered? And, is it to your advantage to tackle now or to wait patiently for another chance?

Techniques

The technique for tackling from the front is a series of simple steps. Time the tackle to coincide with the instant the opponent is going to

play the ball. His foot will already be committed, as will the direction and force of his dribble. Strike the tackling foot through the center of the ball, placing the nontackling foot to one side and behind the ball. As you make contact, shift your weight onto the supporting leg and block the ball with the inside of your foot, knees bent to absorb the shock of meeting the ball and possibly the charge of your opponent. Bending the knees also lowers your center of gravity and makes it more difficult for you to be knocked over by the impact.

Wedge the ball with your foot and then lift or roll it out. A shoulder charge is an effective part of the tackle, although you are tackling the ball and not the man.

To tackle from the side, follow most of these steps, but now you will be chasing from behind or to the side and should attempt to get the nontackling foot even with or slightly in front of the ball before you pivot your body and block the ball.

The sliding tackle is dangerous, because if you miss the ball you have taken yourself out of play by falling down; or, if you miss the ball, you stand a good chance of tripping your opponent and receiving a penalty. You must try to get as near as possible to the ball. As you approach the ball, veer slightly so that your line of slide will take you across the path of the ball. If you make contact with the ball first and the player falls, it is still a legal contact as long as you were legitimately playing the ball and not the man.

Common Mistakes

Common mistakes in tackling are: the tackler lunges at the ball; tackles timidly; fails to apply pressure on the ball; and (in the side tackle) commits himself to the tackler when he is behind the ball rather than even with it.

Drills

Individual competition against an attacker is the best way to practice tackling. The attacker should work the ball in different positions on the field and should employ a variety of techniques and feints to test your tackling prowess.

8
Goal Keeping

Responsibilities

In soccer's early history, the slowest or the least skilled player was always picked as a goalkeeper. In 1897 Sheffield United of England had a goalkeeper who weighed 320 pounds. But the goalkeeper is the most important player on the field in modern soccer. He must have quick reflexes and sure hands as well as courage and athletic talent —like Lev Yachine of Russia, who was once described as having "telescopic arms," and who, with Gordon Banks of England, was the most renowned goalkeeper of the last 20 years.

The goalkeeper is the last defender and the first attacking player. When he has the ball safe in his hands, it is totally at rest. No one can take it from him. For this reason, the goalkeeper is in the strategic position of being able to scan the field and initiate a counterattack with a quick pass to an open man. He must be a field player involved in all play.

Body Position

An aspiring goalkeeper first learns correct body position. Your feet should be about shoulder's width apart, knees slightly bent, hands away from the side with the palms facing the field of play. In this crouch, you are ready and able to move in any direction. Girls who have had gymnastic training will especially appreciate how important initial body position and stance are for moving quickly and gracefully to make a save.

In most instances, the following principles apply for stopping a shot:

1. The body should always be behind the ball. This prevents the ball from slipping through the arms.

2. On an overhead shot, you should jump high enough to back the ball with the chest.

3. Catch the ball using both hands, fingers spread wide, but relaxed.

4. As you catch the ball, withdraw the hands or body, or both, to absorb the force of the shot so it won't bounce away—a rebound provides an attacker with a cheap goal.

Against hard shots at stomach level, the goalkeeper takes a little backward hop to cushion the impact. Watch the ball until it is clasped securely in your stomach. Always pull the ball into the stomach to avoid having it slip free. The main point is to always get your body behind the ball, especially on wet or cold days when your hands may betray you.

Different shots require different reactions by the goalkeeper. Fielding low shots is the goalkeeper's hardest task. To pick up hard ground shots, move your body behind the ball, ankles together, knees straight, and bend from the waist as the ball rolls toward you. Spread your fingers, hands down, little fingers together, and pick up the ball in front of your feet.

An alternate method is to align the feet and bend one knee sideways to the oncoming ball. The sideways placement prevents the knee from jutting out and bumping the ball back onto the field. Twist the upper body to face the shot. Prepare to receive the ball with your hands down, palms upward. The hands are again spread with the two little fingers almost touching. Tuck the elbows and cradle the ball with your arms and stomach. This kneeling position with no gaps between the legs presents a large stopping surface and forces you to bring your eyes down close to the ball's line of flight.

On a shot directly at the chest, make the save in front of the body. With thumbs together, catch the ball with a strong grip, giving just a bit to cushion it.

On high spots, place your hands behind the ball, palms in, and jump off the foot closest to the goal line. Catch the ball at its highest point. As soon as you grab it, bring it into the chest. Step toward the ball before you jump. The forward momentum will help you jump a little higher.

Tipping and Punching

Always try to catch and hold the ball rather than tip or punch it away. Tipping and punching, however, are sometimes necessary for balls that cannot be caught. Tip the ball with that part of the palm of the hand just below the fingers, rather than with the lower palm or the fist. Your fingers are longer and provide better control in directing the deflection of the ball. If the ball is at the crossbar, play it with your palms facing the field and tip it over the top of the goal.

There are many times when a ball cannot be safely caught because the goalkeeper is surrounded by opposing players. In a crowd, the goalkeeper must be able to leap and punch the ball away. The safest method is to hammer the ball with two hands, fists together. Punch the ball at the top of your jump. Always hit the ball to the side of the field, never up the middle. On high hard shots, you may want to tip or punch the ball away if you are unsure about catching it. Safety is the best policy.

Reducing the Angle

The first rule of thumb against a shooter is to try to narrow the angle of the shot to present the attacker with the smallest possible target. By coming out of the goal on the side of the ball, you obstruct the shooter's view of the goal. The more you advance toward him, the larger the area of goal you block from his sight. This is known as cutting the angle. To learn the laws of angle play, tie two ropes, one to each goalpost. Extend the ropes until they are taut. Holding the two loose ends, walk in a semicircle from one side of the goal front to the other. You will walk in an arc, and at any point along the arc you will be able to stop and study the dimensions of the goal and the two boundary lines of flight, marked by the ropes, in which the attacker must propel the ball toward the goal. The goalkeeper who remains riveted to the goal line gives the attacker most of the goal to shoot at—a broad target that good shooters do not miss.

There are risks involved in coming out of the goal. You have to know how far you can advance and still cover the sides with short dives. If you come too far too soon, the forward with the ball may pass to another player. If you venture too far, the forward may try to lob the ball overhead. Approach the ball under control to prevent the attacker from feinting and dribbling by you. Occasionally, against a forward who has dribbled too far in front or temporarily lost control of the ball, a pantherlike move by the goalkeeper to fall on the ball will be effective. Experienced goalkeepers patrol the penalty area with a vengeance, not only cutting off shots but intercepting lead passes between opposing forwards.

You can further limit the chance of a score by forcing attackers to the side of the goal. This requires some feinting on your part. If you know, for example, that the attacker is a right-footed kicker—and you should know because it is part of the goalkeeper's job—overplay him in such a way that he will have to move left and shoot with his weaker foot.

Diving

As part of your acrobatic performance in the goal you may have to dive after a ball to catch it or tip it away. You needn't worry about making an Olympic dive; just concentrate on saving the shot. Face the ball, bend your legs as if they were springs, then push off, falling sideways, with your body behind the ball, hands outstretched for the ball. The full extension of the body on the ground serves as a long wall to block the shot. As the ball is retrieved and pulled into the stomach, roll over toward the opponent and fold your head, arms, and knees to your stomach, hugging the ball to protect it and yourself. Always dive sideways. A forward dive toward the opponent exposes your head to the kicker's foot.

Ball Possession

Once the ball is caught, the goalkeeper faces a new set of challenges. It is a rule that you cannot take more than 4 steps without bouncing the ball. An opponent may station himself in front of your kicking foot and force you to kick wrong-footed.

Distributing Passes

Distributing the ball to a free man is another important function of goal keeping. Once you save the ball, don't just punt it upfield. A long, high kick has a good chance of being recovered by the other team.

The most accurate way to deliver the ball is by throwing it one of several ways: overarm or sidearm like a baseball player; underarmed as in bowling; or stiffarmed as in cricket bowling. Short, accurate throws made quickly are better than long throws that require more time to launch and give the other team extra seconds to anticipate the direction of the pass. Rolled balls are easiest of all to control.

The goalkeeper needs to master the basic kicking techniques, since he will often push a quick pass to a teammate, boot a long ball off the ground, dropkick, and punt the ball with either foot. The punt is employed mostly to relieve pressure on the goal and to vary the tempo of the game. The drop-kick, struck just as it bounces on the ground, is designed to get the ball upfield under control. Most goalkeepers of any merit can drop-kick to within 10–15 feet of a target. This kick travels in a lower trajectory than the punt and is more effective against a stiff wind.

On out-of-bounds plays over the goal line, the goalkeeper rather than a defender, should take the goal kick. When a defender falls back to kick, he removes himself from the field of play; his team is minus one man in its own sector until he can resume his position.

Controlling the Defense

The final role of the goalkeeper is that of controlling the defense, talking to the defenders, calling attention to developing situations, to problems, sudden advantages, etc. The goalkeeper can see the entire field of play, while a defender focuses on only a single segment.

Common Errors

The most common errors a goalkeeper makes are: he catches too many "easy" balls with hands only; fields low balls with legs open; adds pressure to the defense by not venturing out to catch high balls; plays angles poorly; stays on the line; doesn't study the attacking teams; and punts the ball away carelessly.

Drills

To practice against balls that are hit above the knee, or above extended arms, two goalkeepers stand facing each other about five to eight yards apart. Each takes turn volley punting the ball back and forth to one another. Aim high, low, right, left, and at midsection of the target. Concentrate on catching the ball with both hands, grabbing it, holding on, and then withdrawing the ball into the cradle of your arms. Punt harder until each of you has had considerable practice at stopping high-speed balls.

Change your position now to that of sitting with your legs extended about ten yards from another goalkeeper, who stands. The standing goalkeeper throws balls to all different sides of your body. Catch each ball using proper technique, and then return it to the serving goalkeeper with the correct upper-body throwing form.

Another exercise is to stand in the center of the goal. The second goalkeeper serves 2 rolling balls alternately to each post. Make the save, return it to the server, and then go immediately to the other post to stop the next ball. A variation of this drill is for the server to put the ball in the air toward each post.

Another good drill for reflexes is to stand facing a wall, 3–4 yards off. A server plays a ball against a wall and you must make the save as it rebounds.

Stand in the goal and have several players take shots (at 12–15 yards) from different angles and at different speeds and heights. Concentrate on form, quickness, and catching.

To learn how to dive, practice falling from a kneeling position into hay or foam rubber. Do not fall on your elbows, but land on your upper back in a sideways rolling motion—shoulders first, hips next. When you are familiar with the body roll, move to a squatting position, then on to a half-standing, and finally, a full standing position.

9
Functional Training

Definition

To improve your ability as a player, concentrate on the basic skills; but also practice the duties of the position you play. Practice for your role on a team is what we mean by functional training. Such training describes a logical progression from individual exercises to match-related conditions to actual game situations.

Responsibilities of Different Positions

The general responsibilities of the different positions in soccer are as follows: The *defender* plays individual or combination defense against the opposition's attackers to prevent goals, and also supports his own offense by initiating a counterattack. The *midfielder,* the player who requires the best all-around skills in the game today, links the defense to the attack and falls back into the defense to help with tackling, guarding opponents, and with the transition of the ball from the opponent's attack to his team's possession. When his team resumes its attack, the midfielder supports the forwards and is prepared to pass or shoot on goal. The *forward's* job is to beat opponents, to score goals and, equally important, to be the first line of defense when the opponents have the ball. The *goalkeeper* stops shots, prevents goals, and starts an offensive thrust whenever possible.

Defense

In its most basic form, defense is a matter of one individual trying to prevent another from scoring a goal. The first line of duty is to check your opponent. These 4 guidelines will help you play tight, resourceful defense against any attacker:

1. When the ball is free or in contention, the defender has to fight for the ball and attempt to win it.

2. The best time to try to steal the ball is when the opponent has just received an incoming ball and does not have it under full control.

3. This principle takes effect if the attacker has settled the ball and begins to press forward. Never let the person with the ball get behind you. If necessary, give ground to maintain a cushion between you and him and to delay him until you can steal the ball or intercept his pass. Watch the ball, stay balanced (don't cross your legs), and wait for the chance to tackle the ball.

If your opponent does not have possession, keep him and the ball in sight, covering for your fellow defenders, and remaining close enough to your own opponent to prevent him from getting a direct pass. In general terms, the closer your opponent is to the ball, the tighter he is marked. Man-to-man marking changes to a zone defense away from the ball.

If the attackers outnumber you two to one, as often happens, keep both players in sight, retreat so as to prevent a through pass, and wait until help arrives. The maximum retreating distance is normally the penalty area line, 18 yards out, the beginning of the shooting range for most young players. When you reach this line, you must take a stand and challenge the ball.

4. Make your opponent do what you want him to. If he is going to shoot at the goal, he is going to have to earn that opportunity.

The most common mistake a defender makes is to rush a player who has the ball in his possession overaggressively and allow himself to be beaten either by a dribble or a through pass. Good defenders know when to attack and tackle with force and when to play more cautious cat-and-mouse delaying tactics.

What happens if an attacker beats you? Frequently, the defender will turn and give chase. That is wrong. You should run back toward the goal mouth along the shortest path to the goal. In a well-organized defense, someone will have moved over to intercept your opponent (this is why good defensive players cover for each other as well as guard their own opponents), and now you must locate his opponent who may well be standing free in the goal area.

Drills for Defenders

Practice clearing the ball without pressure from an opponent. Stand on the edge of the 6-yard box and have someone serve you balls from a variety of angles, heights, and directions. Unmolested for now by an opponent, clear the ball upfield by directing it back to the server, by passing long to forwards, and by guiding it to the goalkeeper, who is always your best ally. The principles of ball control remain the same. Don't just boot the ball; direct it to a teammate. Practice heading, and kicking with both feet

The next level is to do this exercise under pressure. Now you bring on line your skill at winning balls in contention. Against a single attacker, try to head or kick balls tossed to you by a server, upfield to a teammate. The server delivers the ball to both you and a forward who battles you for possession. A variation is to have several forwards rush you each time you receive the ball. Play the ball back to the server, either at his feet or up high, however the server designates.

In the next phase, the server passes to an offensive player positioned five yards from you. Try to steal the ball before the forward settles it.

Another useful way to practice retrieving balls that have penetrated the defensive zone is to turn your back and play facing the goal. Stand near the touchline with a server who rolls the ball down into the corner so that you chase it with your back to the field of play. When you retrieve the ball, turn it upfield and pass to an open teammate or to the goalkeeper. Do this without pressure, then progress to working against opposition with a forward racing at your heels.

Against an attacker who has already settled the ball, stand 10 yards outside the penalty area and play the attacker straight on employing the principles of good defense. The attacker tries to beat you for a shot. You attempt to force him outside and, at the right moment, steal or tackle the ball. A variation of this is to have the attacker move laterally along the penalty area, employing feints to bypass you for a shot on goal.

Progress from this level to work against overloaded attacks in which you are outnumbered, and finally to actual game situations where, with the help of your goalkeeper, you both defend and begin a counterattack. The mark of an all-around defender is the ability to instigate an attack with one sudden, swift pass, after beating the opposing attacker for the ball.

Midfielders

Midfield play is probably the most vital factor in the success of a soccer team. Probably the most important role is to prepare the attack. Expert passing, excellent conditioning, and a total knowledge of the game are requisites for this position. If the midfield player holds the ball too long, the chance for an attack may be missed. On the other hand, if he doesn't hold it long enough the attack may never form. The predominant midfielders today have inexhaustible stamina and skill at all aspects of the game.

Fundamental skills for midfielders in the offensive sector of the field include the abilities to pass ground balls over long distances to forwards; to cross the ball from one zone of the field to another; to split the defense with perfectly timed passes; to shoot long range from 20–30 yards out with speed and accuracy; and to dribble. These skills can be developed through the drills described in the appropriate sections of this book.

Drills for Midfielders

To learn when to hold the ball and when to advance it, two midfielders play against a single defender. The defender guards the midfielder without the ball, while the passer tries to anticipate when his teammate will break free to receive the ball. Midfielders should switch positions in this drill, since the exercise of learning how to beat the defender to receive a pass is also of value. A word about playing off the ball—it is as important to know what to do without the ball as it is with it. Receivers have as much responsibility for insuring effective, safe passes as do the passers themselves.

The next building block involves 3 attackers against a single defender. The defender still marks a forward without the ball. The midfielders use interpassing while looking for the through pass to the forward. This drill helps build coordination between midfielders and also shows the value of switching the ball across the field to open up different passing lanes.

To re-create match conditions, use a 3 versus 2 situation; one midfielder takes the ball, one midfielder plays off the ball, shadowed by a defender, and one forward, also closely guarded, tries to get open. The unmarked midfielder tries to pass the ball off, then penetrates the inner defense to receive a return pass and shoot.

Other variations include a group contest in which 5 midfielders and forwards compete against 4 defenders in the offensive zone. Each midfielder works to free himself for a pass with the stipulation that every second or third pass must be to a midfielder. Each time a midfielder receives the ball, he must dribble it a specified number of times or bypass an opponent before he can lay the ball off to a teammate. This exercise develops a sense of team cooperation and a knowledge of how to play away from the ball.

Practice through passes by joining with 2 other midfielders against 2 defenders on a half field, keeping in mind the offsides rule. Play the ball laterally from one midfielder to another. The object is to strike at the gaps that open for an instant between the 2 defenders as they shift about to cover your passes. When the defenders become flat, or lose the ability to back each other up, you should split them with a pass to a teammate who on cue has sprinted by his defender to gather the ball behind the defender. Practice this with 4 attackers against 3 defenders, and with 6 versus 4.

Midfielders have a tendency to play exclusively on one side of the field. Failure to use the broad front of the entire offensive sector will seriously limit the attack. Change the direction of attack in two ways, either with a square pass to a midfielder in a zone adjacent to you, or by chipping the ball over the defense to a player crossfield. Also, when play is crowded in your area, don't forget the value of using your defenders to open up the attack; they are often of great help in adding to the offense.

The final item in an attacking midfielder's vast array of tricks and devices is scoring effectiveness. Set up a drill where you try to shoot from 20–30 yards out in front of the goal, first unguarded, then with a defender. Shoot quickly, forcefully, and accurately at the goalposts. Bang the ball hard from this far distance, but don't sacrifice accuracy. Have a forward pass the ball to you and shoot the rolling ball. Many of your game shots will be balls sent back to you by forwards in front or to the side of you.

So far, techniques and drills have pertained to midfielders supporting the attack. When possession of the ball is lost in the offensive zone, the midfielder reverts immediately to defense and brings all the principles of individual defense to bear on regaining the ball. For individual skills, see the appropriate chapters.

One important difference between a defender and a midfielder is that the midfielder is not the last line of defense. You can afford, therefore, to be aggressive and give chase to the ball right away. That's one tactic. A second one is to fall back and delay the attack by giving the defense, if it has been caught out of position, time to regroup, or by trying to befuddle the opposition, jamming its offensive zone with excessive players.

In addition to the specific midfield drills mentioned, normal functional training for midfielders is to split their practice time between attack and defense routines.

One further note about midfield play concerns throw-ins. Since midfielders cover the length of the field, more often than not they are closest to an out-of-bounds ball and thus are the best people to make the throw-in quickly and advantageously. Aspiring midfielders should learn this game skill well.

A mistake that midfielders commonly make is to play with the head down and not use teammates. A midfielder who becomes too engrossed in beating a defender or overdribbling limits his effectiveness. Another fault is wasteful running. Do not chase around the field trying to do too much; pace yourself to assist with offense and help with defense.

Forwards

The main criterion for a forward is the ability to put the ball in the back of the net. Goal scoring is a great talent. Alfredo di Stefano, the "White Arrow" of Real Madrid, scored 460 goals in 622 matches for Spain, but none of his goals were more astounding than the one he sent whistling into the nets in the 1960 European Cup final from 2 paces beyond the center circle—half the length of the field! Another example—Pelé, in 1958 World Cup play, in the penalty box, with his back to the goal, received a high crossing pass on his thigh. He lobbed a kick over his head against the body of the defender, whirled, and struck home a goal before the ball had touched the ground. Brute strength, incomparable dexterity—such talents must be developed through diligent practice, not only of the basic skills of shooting and ball control, but against all the challenges of match conditions. You can't just stand in front of a goal with a dozen balls and shoot. You must act out the entire scenario—from the point when you first free yourself from a defender to when you sight the ball on target and score.

The chance for prolonged individual competition between a forward and a defender in the heavy traffic of the inner defense is rare.

Consequently, forwards, as was stressed with midfielders, should constantly practice man-up advantages, particularly 2 attackers versus a single defender.

There are certain fundamentals that forwards must know. Knowing how to play without the ball is one. Many scoring opportunities are lost by forwards standing and watching a teammate with the ball rather than moving into the open spaces left by the defense. This responsibility parallels in importance that of knowing how to anticipate when a teammate is about to free himself and how to pass the ball to an area where he can run to retrieve it unmolested.

Another point is to avoid offside infractions by making every pass near the goal area, accurate and timely, and in such a manner that it cannot be intercepted by a defender or the goalkeeper.

In man-advantage situations, there are many variables that must be repeated over and over to insure reasonable success in a game.

Wall Pass

Probably the most effective way for two attackers to beat a lone defender is by use of the wall pass, also known as a one-two, a double pass, and a give and go.

In the wall pass (see Diagram 1), the attacker, A, with the ball, takes on the defender, D, directly. As you, A, approach D, the supporting player, S, your teammate, positions himself to help you, facing you at a right angle to the direction you are running. On receiving a pass from A, S turns his foot out as if it were part of a low wall and uses it to deflect a pass from you with one touch at such an angle that the ball will roll behind D. As soon as you pass to S, run behind D to gather the return pass (see Diagram 2). The return pass is hit quickly to beat D and also prevent the possibility of A running to an offside position.

The most common mistake in a wall pass is to try to cover too large an area with the passes. Also, S may stand so far ahead of you that he narrows the passing lane. Another error is for S to deflect the ball too far ahead into the range of another defender or the goalkeeper.

There are many options, depending on the reaction of D. If D overplays you, then you can pass quickly to S and run by D. If D shades S, making a pass to him risky, fake the wall pass and take a shot. After you have passed to S, if D follows you closely and prevents

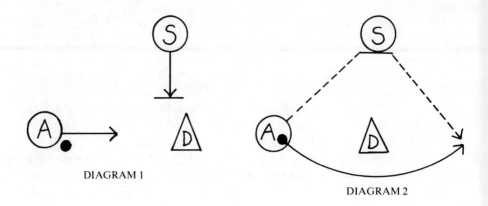

DIAGRAM 1

DIAGRAM 2

DIAGRAM 3

DIAGRAM 4

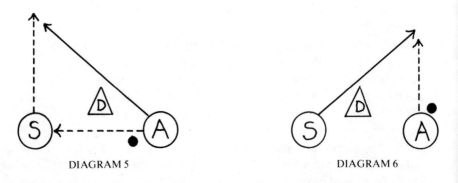

DIAGRAM 5

DIAGRAM 6

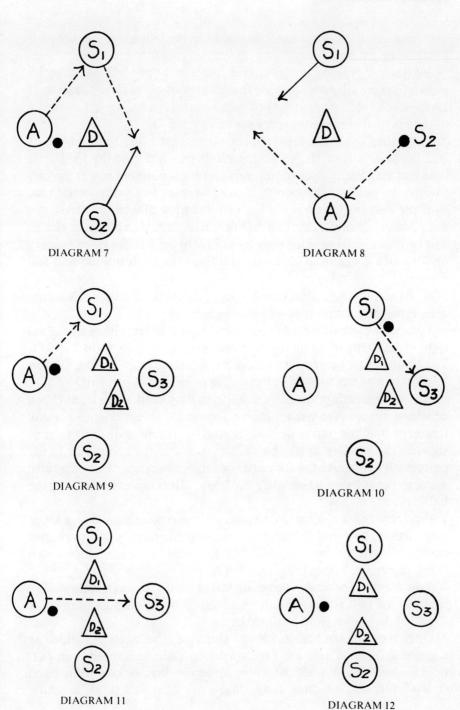

DIAGRAM 7

DIAGRAM 8

DIAGRAM 9

DIAGRAM 10

DIAGRAM 11

DIAGRAM 12

you from getting open, then S should keep the ball and either shoot or pass elsewhere.

A different type of wall pass features S in front of D, as though S were a basketball center playing the pivot with his back to the goal. If D plays behind S, pass to S, who runs to meet the ball and then taps it to the side you are running (see Diagrams 3 and 4).

Two other 2 versus 1 drills for forwards are the square through pass and the lateral run. In the first, pass squarely across the field to S, then run diagonally upfield to receive a return ball that is sent directly toward the goal—a through pass (see Diagram 5). On the lateral run, stop the ball then push it through to S cutting diagonally across the field behind the defender. S must not run too sharp an angle, or else he will be blocked from your pass by D or will be offsides (see Diagram 6). Practice 2 against 1 drills constantly, both with limited and full defense.

Drills employing 3 attackers against 1 defender are helpful learning aids, especially for playing without the ball.

You have the ball with 2 supporters, S_1 and S_2, on either side. Pass right or left depending on the movement of D (see Diagrams 7 and 8). The timing must be precise to avoid offsides and interception. Give to S_1 who then passes to S_2, if he has gotten open, or back to you.

An excellent adaption of this drill is to play keep-away from D in a confined space. Against untrained forwards, an experienced D will intercept half the passes because S_1 and S_2 will mistime their runs or shorten the passing angles by failing to move far enough or in the correct direction. As the forwards become more conscious of how to move to open spaces D should have less and less success in stealing the ball.

Four attackers against 2 defenders is the next step. Playing keep-away again, you and 2 supporters, S_1 and S_2, move open to receive passes while trying to spread D_1 and D_2 to make a through pass to a third teammate, S_3 (see Diagrams 9–12).

You cannot practice these different drills enough times. The majority of failures in a mature goal attack occur because of misplay in one of these situations outlined here.

Once the forward has decided to shoot, all the factors of shooting come into play. These are explained in detail in Chapter 6. In particular, you should practice turning and shooting, kicking rolling and flying balls, and heading. Individual work against a single defender with emphasis on shooting off the dribble is also necessary. Forwards must be able to beat their defenders in a confined space. Place 4 cones or markers on the field just outside the penalty area, forming a 10-yard square. Two defenders, one in front of the other, are stationed in the square. The ball is served to you. Take on the first defender within the allotted space. After beating him, take on the second defender, defeat him, and shoot on goal.

Place a cone or shirt 25 yards out in front of the goal and station yourself by it. Two servers, each with several balls, stand on both sides of the field alternatively serving balls across the face of the goal, just outside the 6-yard box. Run to the ball and shoot at first touch, sprint back around the cone, and return to shoot the ball on the opposite side. The passes should be timed so you are in constant motion.

Forwards are not excused from defensive responsibilities by any means. When ball possession is lost upfield, you immediately chase the ball if you are nearest to it. If you are on the other side of the field, fall back to stop outlet passes. Aggressive, tight marking in the offensive side of the field relieves the midfielders and defenders of having to come too far upfield to defend, and provides the defense time to settle.

The most frequent error by forwards is to hurry the attack unnaturally. As soon as another attacker gets the ball, inexperienced or overanxious forwards sprint for the goal. This can cause pressure on the passer, who must risk an interception to make a through pass, and it can place the eager forward in an offsides position. Patience in building up the attack is a virtue. The other most common mistake is to shoot the ball too hard. Accuracy is your first concern.

Goalkeepers

Individual techniques and drills are covered extensively in Chapter 8. Functional training for goalkeepers means placing a goalkeeper under pressure not only as a saver of shots but as a complete field player.

Twelve or fewer players stand 18–20 yards out from the goal in a semicircle. Each has a ball. One after another, as the goalkeeper readies himself, each player kicks the ball with speed and accuracy on goal. The goalkeeper tries to save every shot. Since this is mostly an exercise to help the goalkeeper speed up his reactions, it's important for the shooters not to let the goalkeeper get completely set. The peppering of shots should cover the entire goal mouth to make the goalkeeper move about. A variation of this drill is to screen the goalkeeper with a line of players. Place 1 or 2 players directly in front of the goal to obstruct the goalkeeper's vision. The attackers shoot right at this human wall, which then either moves or ducks to let the ball whiz by, or else tries to deflect the ball into the goal corner.

A goalkeeper must work against crossing passes and corner kicks, deciding whether to catch, punch, or tip the ball—techniques outlined earlier in the book.

Servers should loft long passes from all directions to teammates waiting in front of the goal so that the goalkeeper learns to be alert to all invaders of his territory. A frequent mistake by a goalkeeper is to turn and face a crossing shot or corner kick directly. In such a position, he is blind to any penetration behind his back. He should face such kicks at an angle so that he can scan all of the immediate goal area in which the incoming ball is going to land. The 6-yard box is his domain, and he must patrol it vigilantly.

Goalkeepers must practice against breakaways. By feinting and faking, try to force the onrushing attacker to the side of the goal to reduce the angle of his shot and to make him shoot hurriedly and less carefully.

When the goalkeeper is not involved directly in drills on goal, he should practice on the field so that he acquires all the skills of a field player as well as a complete knowledge of tactics, including counterattack strategy.

10
Physical Training

Definition

In the preface, it was pointed out that physical training is not yet something to which you should devote large amounts of time. Your concern now must be to develop the basic soccer skills. A word or two should be said, however, about the types of physical training employed in soccer for the benefit of those interested in the principles of endurance and speed and in improving these aspects of their game.

If you have endurance, you are able to participate effectively in activities such as soccer over a prolonged period of time at varying rates of intensity. Along with endurance, you need speed, agility, power, and flexibility, for soccer's essential activities require total body effort. You have to run with and without the ball on an average of 4–7 miles a game. Many runs are spurts of high speed over 10–20 yard distances. Constant stopping and starting exacts high amounts of energy from the body. Your movements also include quick turns, jumping, heading, twisting, weaving, and dodging. While all of this physical activity is underway, the brain is also functioning in high gear, as each player tries to anticipate and outwit his opponent.

In a poorly conditioned player, the onset of fatigue occurs early and is obvious; his performance begins to deteriorate fast, especially if game conditions are less than perfect—too hot, too cold, too windy, or something. Poor conditioning affects play, decreases the chance of winning, and increases the risk of injury.

The opposite holds true, too. The more endurance you have, the speedier and stronger you are, the better your chances are for success. While you cannot always control the bounce of the ball, you can influence the degree of your conditioning and its effect on your play.

Fortunately, many drills in soccer can be adapted to meet the purposes of endurance and conditioning as well as skill development. By varying the speed or the work rate of the majority of drills in this book, you can economically accomplish the objectives of physical training. Listed below are the major types of training. Included also is brief mention of an off-season program.

One further word: when you are ready to begin a formal training program, plan your exercises carefully and let them build in intensity gradually. Set goals for yourself and record your progress. Above all else, do not sacrifice skill development for physical training. Anyone can run without a ball.

Interval Running

Alternate short periods of intense work with brief rest spells to build stamina and speed. For instance, walk 25 yards, jog 25, and then sprint 25. Repeat several times. Jog forward for 25, and then turn and run backwards for 25. Jog for 50, sprint 25, walk and jog again, increasing the distance of your sprint. Another way is to sprint for time, pause 30 seconds, and then run again more slowly, alternating slower and faster sequences with brief rest intervals. Change the distance, time, and repetitions (number of times you run each exercise) as you see fit.

Interval running with the ball adds a double benefit.

Maze Runs or Broken Field Patterns

The purpose of maze runs is to simulate the normal running patterns of a player in a game. Using markers of some sort, create an obstacle course that will help you practice sharp-angled cuts and pivots as you dribble through as fast as you can (without sacrificing ball control).

Pressure Training

Pressure training involves performing several ball skills of one kind or another in rapid succession. For instance, you receive a succession of incoming balls, each of which you must play off with your foot before the next ball arrives. Pressure by opponents is also employed.

Circuit Training

Circuit training is a controlled progression of exercises whose sum effect is very demanding on your body. For instance, in a series of exercises that tax the legs, stomach, arms, and chest in a minimum period of time, any one exercise taken by itself may not prove a strain; but at the end of the prescribed time, when the drills have been completed, the cumulative effect is intense.

Ball Skill Drills

Ball skill exercises concentrate, as the name implies, mainly on skill development. They should not be utilized for physical training until you have mastered the techniques.

Body Strength

A word about body strength. It will increase naturally through constant exercise. Young players should avoid weightlifting of any kind until they are more mature physically and understand fully the correct techniques and purpose of weightlifting, an altogether different science.

Push-ups, sit-ups, wrestling, and leg lifts, are tremendous body builders and will complement your endurance running and skill development.

Off-Season

The importance of an off-season training program should not be overlooked. At your ages, it can be a most profitable time of dedication, one that will benefit you as a player during the next year. It is imperative after the season is over to relax and separate yourself completely from participation in soccer competition. Not only your body but your mind needs a rest from the pressures of match competition. It is important, however, particularly for older players, to maintain good muscular tone, correct body weight, and some degree of endurance for your continued development as a player and your own personal well-being. Follow an informal program of exercise 2 or 3 times a week. Volleyball, basketball, swimming, handball, tennis, and badminton are excellent activities for a change of pace during the in-between season.

You can't, of course, forsake your soccer skills altogether. The off-season is the time to "make hay." You can accomplish a great amount by continuing to practice such skills as trapping, passing, chipping, heading, shooting, and dribbling. Emphasize form and balance without worrying about pressure from an opponent, and then build to the match situations described in this book.

11
Supplemental Drills

Drills 1–40 are done with the ball, and *Drills 41–57* without the ball, to develop soccer fitness—agility, flexibility, power, endurance, and skill. *Drills 58–67* are ball control exercises. *Drills 68–91* are for practice in developing the attack.

1. *Starting Position* (*SP*): Stand, ball in hands. Bounce the ball from the front to the back with one hand. Leave the ball momentarily. Twist around at the waist and continue bouncing the ball around the back to the front with the other hand.

2. *SP:* Sit, legs extended with ball. Roll the ball around the extended legs, behind the body, and to the front with one hand, then the other.

3. *SP:* Stand with ball in hands; bounce the ball with two hands in front of body while hopping up and down, knees bending. *Variation:* Bounce three times, then bounce ball through legs, turn and repeat.

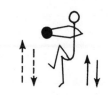

4. *SP:* On stomach with legs and arms extended. Roll back and forth on the stomach while holding the ball extended to the front.

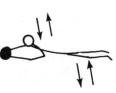

5. *SP:* Sit with ball held in lap. Do a back roll and place ball with hands behind body. Pick up ball with feet and return to starting position.

6. *SP:* Stand with ball next to feet, hop over stationary ball, front to back. *Variation:* Hop over the ball from side to side.

7. *SP:* Front leaning rest position with hands on ball. Do push-ups with hands on ball.

8. *SP:* Stand with ball between heels. Hop up and throw ball over shoulder from back to the front.

9. *SP:* On back with arms and legs extended, holding ball with hands, feet 6 inches off ground. Bring ball over head and knees up to chest. Return to starting position.

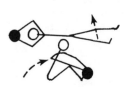

10. *SP:* Sit with ball between feet, legs 6 inches off ground. Move legs with ball over head. Touch the ground with toes, return to starting position.

11. *SP:* Stand with ball in hand; skip in different direction, lifting the knees high and bouncing the ball with hands. *Variation:* Bounce the ball with sole of feet while skipping.

12. *SP:* On back, knees up with ball in hands. Lift the back off floor and roll ball under from one side to other. Lower the back and take ball over the chest. Repeat.

13. *SP:* Stand with ball in hands. Imaginative dribbling with ball, using hands. *Variation:* Imaginative dribbling with ball, using feet.

14. *SP:* Partners stand facing each other 5 yards apart with ball. Toss ball at each other at various angles and at various speeds.

15. *SP:* Partners sit facing each other 5 yards apart with balls. Toss balls at each other at various angles and at various speeds.

16. *SP:* Partners stand facing each other 5 yards apart with balls at feet. Pass balls back and forth to each other with feet.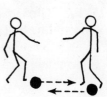

17. *SP:* Partners stand facing each other 5 yards apart with one ball. Player with ball jumps straight up as high as he can, hangs there momentarily, brings feet and ball back, then tosses it to his partner.

18. *SP:* Partners sit facing each other 5 yards apart with ball. Do a back roll bringing ball over the head with hands. Touch it with feet; return to starting position and toss ball to partner, all in one continuous motion.

19. *SP:* Partners stand facing each other 5 yards apart with ball. As in Exercise #17, jump up, hang, then using a volleyball set-up pass, move the ball to the partner.

20. *SP:* Partners on stomach face each other with ball. Bring ball behind head while raising feet and toss to partner. Partner does same.

21. *SP:* Partners stand facing each other 5 yards apart with ball. Ball is placed between feet and tossed to partner. *Variation:* Place ball between heels and toss ball over shoulder to partner.

22. *SP:* Partners stand facing each other holding one ball. One player holds ball tightly while other tries to wrestle ball away from him.

23. *SP:* Three players stand in line 5 yards apart with one ball. Outside man heads ball to middle man who heads to other outside man. Ball is returned to middle, etc.

24. *SP:* Stand, ball at feet. Dribble in a relaxed manner, then push the ball ahead of you and sprint after it quickly. Continue this for a period of time.

25. *SP:* Stand with ball at feet, juggle ball with thigh, with feet, and with head. Then volley ball 5–10 yards away and sprint after it. Concentrate on proper trapping as well!

26. *SP:* Sit with ball in hands. Toss ball to feet, instep kick over the shoulder; get up quickly and trap down the ball on the first bounce.

27. *SP:* Stand with ball in hands. Toss or kick ball up, sit down, get up, and trap the ball before it touches the ground. *Variation:* Instead of sitting, do a forward, backward roll.

28. *SP:* Stand with legs apart and back to the goal. Ball is passed between legs. Player turns quickly and sprints to ball then shoots at goal. *Variation:* Player faces goal.

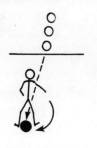

29. *SP:* Players line up facing the goal with ball. Single wall passing. Ball is passed directly at partner who moves directly to ball. Passer cuts quickly for goal after making pass and receives return pass for a shot on goal.

30. Split jumps. *SP:* Stand without ball; hop 2 times, jump up, split legs forward and back. Land with feet together. Ten splits x 2 rebounds.

31. Push-ups. *SP:* Front leaning rest position. Do normal push-ups 30 times. Hold in bent position for 7 seconds (count to 11).

32. Knee lifters. *SP:* Stand without ball. Same as Exercise #30, only lift knees as high as possible. Ten jumps, rest; 2 series.

33. Scissor leg lifts. *SP:* Sit with knees locked and legs off the ground. Move legs up and down 30 times. Then hold legs off ground for 7 seconds (count to 11).

34. Jackknives. *SP:* Sit with knees locked, lift legs 10 times, parallel to ground and reach down and touch toes.

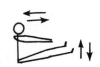

35. Leg crossovers. *SP:* Sit with knees locked, feet off the ground. Move legs to side then cross 30 times.

36. Jump headers. *SP:* Standing. Jump straight up, hang there, bring feet and head back then "head" imaginary ball. Repeat 10 times.

37. Body risers. *SP:* On back. Lift body and knees 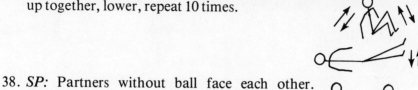 up together, lower, repeat 10 times.

38. *SP:* Partners without ball face each other. Shadow box 3 rounds, 1 minute box, 1 minute rest.

39. *SP:* One partner in crouch position, hands on knees, legs spread. Other partner stands behind. Player standing leaps over partner then crawls back under partner's legs 10 times. Reverse position, other partner leaps.

40. *SP:* Sit with ball between legs 6 inches off ground. Move legs in direction sideways and twist body in opposite direction. *Variation:* Bring knees up to chest keeping ball between feet.

41. *SP:* Stand facing each other holding hands. Turn in same direction so backs are touching then continue turning so partners are facing each other again.

42. *SP:* Stand bent over head to head holding hands. Rotate side to side.

43. *SP:* Stand facing each other with extended arms holding hands. Push against each other forcing arms to the side and chest touching.

44. *SP:* Stand back to back with arms locked. One partner bends over lifting the other off his feet.

45. *SP:* One partner stands and holds thighs of the other partner, whose hands touch the ground. Player standing grabs partner under stomach, around legs, and lifts him over his thighs. *Variation:* Lift, hold, then slowly lower.

46. *SP:* Stand facing each other. Jump, chest against chest at highest point of jump, like heading. *Variation:* Without jumping.

47. *SP:* One player holds partner behind neck while partner holds him under armpits and swings him in a circle.

48. *SP:* Stand facing each other, holding hands tightly. Partners try to touch each other's feet.

49. *SP:* Stand facing each other, one with hands raised parallel to ground; other with hands by his side. First player falls toward other, who pushes him upright, palms extended.

50. *SP:* Back to back, holding hands over each other's head. One partner rolls the other over his back and head.

51. *SP:* Stand facing each other, right foot against other's right foot, right hands holding each other. Partners try to make each other lose their balance.

52. *SP:* Squat position facing each other, holding hands. Partners shuffle their feet and perform the "Russian Dance." *Variation:* Try to push partners off balance, legs on same side.

53. *SP:* Shoulder against shoulder, while hopping on one foot.

54. *SP:* One player stands with partner's feet resting on his shoulders and hands on ground. Do push-ups.

55. *SP:* Sit back to back with arms interlocked. Move from sitting to standing to sitting position against each other.

56. *SP:* Stand facing each other. Try to slap each other's backside.

57. *SP:* One player stands with arms stiff at his sides. Partner crouches behind. Partner tries to lift the player off his feet.

58. Didi Feint. *SP:* Lock ball exactly over the achilles tendon of left heel with inside or outside toe, flip ball over shoulder with left heel.

59. Pivot flick. *SP:* Place right foot beside the ball, shift weight to left foot, and flick with right foot scissors movement.

60. Pivot heel flick. *SP:* Same action as above, scissor movement with heel to move ball backwards.

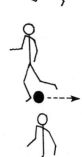

61. Kick blind and go. *SP:* Same as above, only fake the pivot heel kick and bring the foot over the ball and draw it forward with instep.

62. Throw-ins. *SP:* Players line up on the outside edge of penalty area and the goal line. Bend back like a bow. Practice with medicine ball, throw, and follow through by falling down.

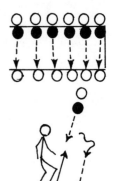

63. Turn and shoot. *SP:* Player receiving the ball goes to meet it, turns and shoots.

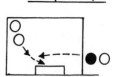

64. Centering, control, shoot. *SP:* Ball is crossed, controlled, and shot.

65. Chipping, control, shoot. *SP:* Ball is chipped back the length of field and shot.

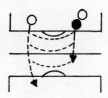

66. Passing, weaving, shoot. *SP:* Ball is passed the length of the field with exchange of positions and shot.

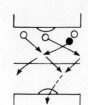

67. One v. one penalty area. *SP:* Competition for the ball chipped into the area from various angles by another player.

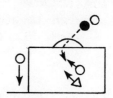

68. Feint left, go right. *SP:* Keep body weight to left side and carry ball to the left with sole of right foot. Feint left then, with increase of speed, take ball to right with inside of left foot.

69. Feint shot or pass, go right. *SP:* Feint shot or pass with right foot by moving foot over ball. Draw ball back with right sole and carry ball to the right side with inside of right foot.

70. Feint shot or pass, go left. *SP:* Feint shot or pass with right foot by moving foot over ball. Draw ball back with right sole, then push ball between legs and behind left leg to left side.

71. Feint back pass, go right. *SP:* Swing right leg over ball with toes up. Hit ball back with heel against the inside of left foot. Ball travels to the right.

72. Drag left, go right. *SP:* Move ball with inside of right foot to the left side. Then quickly draw the ball back to the right side with the outside of the right foot.

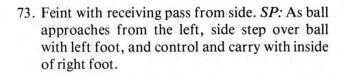

73. Feint with receiving pass from side. *SP:* As ball approaches from the left, side step over ball with left foot, and control and carry with inside of right foot.

74. Shadow Dribbling. *SP:* Partners, each with ball. Leader dribbles and partner follows him, performing the same type of movements.

75. *SP:* Partners each with ball. Both players dribble ball and at some time, try to kick opponent's ball from him without leaving his own ball.

76. *SP:* Four players, 1 ball. Two players act as goal with legs spread apart. Two players, playing for 1 minute on 30-yard area. Players alternate after 1 minute.

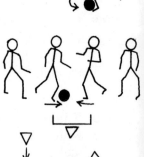

77. *SP:* Two players, 1 ball, and 1 goalkeeper. Ball is tossed into penalty area. Defensive player comes from goal line. Offensive player, from outside penalty area.

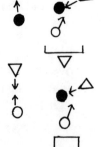

78. *SP:* Two players, 1 ball, 1 goalkeeper in large goal, 1 small goal. Ball is tossed into middle of 10-yard area. Play until goal is scored or time elapsed.

79. *SP:* Two players, 1 ball, restricted boundaries. Player with ball tries to keep ball away from opponent.

80. *SP:* Three players, 1 ball. Player with ball dribbles it. Second player tries to get it. Third player rests. Once second player gets ball, third player challenges, and first player rests. Repeat.

81. *SP:* Three players, 1 ball. Player with ball passes and exchanges positions with receiver at top speed. Receiver looks before receiving ball, goes to meet pass, controls, then passes to third player and exchanges positions with him. All passes received are rolled with hands.

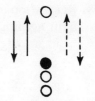

82. Relaxation exercise: 3 minutes. *SP:* 3 players, 1 ball. 5 yards apart in a line. #1 heads to #2 in middle. #2 heads to #1. #1 heads over #2 to #3. Repeat again.

83. *SP:* Same as #14, except basketball chest passes are made instead of rolling the ball back and forth. Look, pass, go. Ten yards interval between.

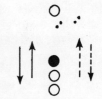

84. Relaxation exercise: 3 minutes. *SP:* 3 players, 1 ball, 5 yards apart in a line. #1 heads to #2. #2 heads over his head behind him to #3; repeat.

85. *SP:* Same as #14, except inside foot passes made. Remember to take first step with foot used in passing, 1 touch.

86. Relaxation exercise: 3 minutes. *SP:* 3 players, 1 ball, 5 yards apart in a triangle. Two touch heading. Jump stop the ball, then head to another player.

87. *SP:* 3 players, 1 ball in confined area. Two offensive players play keep-away from 1 defensive player. If defensive player gets ball, offensive players tries to take it away again.

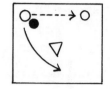

88. Relaxation exercise: 3 minutes. *SP:* 3 players, 1 ball, holding hands in a triangle. Players try to head and juggle ball while holding hands.

89. *SP:* 3 players, 1 ball. Two small goals, confined area. Two offensive players try to score, as does the defensive player if he gets the ball.

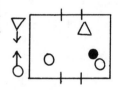

90. Relaxation exercise: 3 minutes. *SP:* 3 players, 1 ball, sit with feet touching in a triangle. Players try to head ball to each other.

91. *SP:* 3 players, 1 goalkeeper, 1 regular goal, 1 small goal, 1 ball and half field. Goalkeeper and defensive player protect large goal. Two offensive players protect small goal.

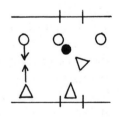

12
Pendulum Training

Pendulum training is a method whereby a soccer ball is suspended at the end of a rope or tether from a pole that is high enough to allow the ball to be kicked to simulate actual flight. Since the ball is captive and swings in a predictable arc, almost every individual skill discussed in this book can be practiced alone, or with a partner, intensively and rapidly.

The ball should be hung from a minimum height of 20 feet on a rope or tether that is adjustable to allow for different-sized players and for the practice of different techniques, such as kicking and heading. About 60 feet of rope is sufficient. The rope can be tied to a tree or hung from a rafter. The best way is to construct a pendulum pole as shown on following page.

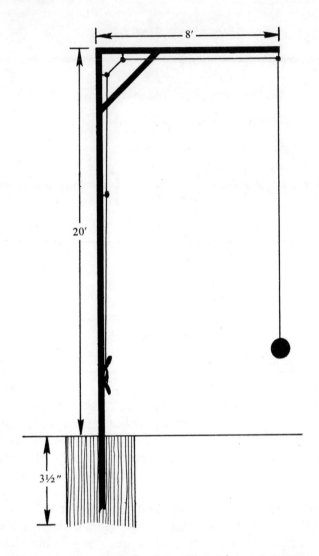

Skills that can be practiced in pendulum training are:

Heading
Stand heading
Jump heading
Trapping with the head
Heading tossed balls
Dive heading
Competition heading (one versus one)

Shooting and Passing

Instep volley
Inside-of-foot volley
Outside-of-foot volley
Side volley
Scissors volley
Outside-of-foot volley

Trapping

Instep
Inside-of-foot
Outside-of-foot
Thigh
Chest
Head
Jump trapping in all areas

Goal Keeping

Punching or boxing
Tipping
Diving
Competition against attacking players

Conclusion

There can be no conclusion to a book about soccer, because there is no end to the evolution of the game itself. The myriad techniques and strategies continue to change and develop.

The focus of this book on individual skills places the emphasis exactly where it belongs, regardless of the level of ability of the individual player. Learn the basic techniques first if you want to become an effective player. The best players in the world always return to the basics. These skills are to be thought of as fundamental tools with which you are provided unlimited scope for creative expression in a game whose blend of artistry and skill has fascinated people the world over for many years.

Glossary

ASL. American Soccer League, oldest professional soccer league in U.S. (1933).

AMATEUR. A player not reimbursed with money for playing.

ATTACKER. Player whose team has ball and is advancing toward goal.

BAR. Crossbar of goal.

BLINDSIDE. Running behind a defender's back.

BODY SWERVE. Use of body fakes and feints to outwit opponent.

BOOKED. To be given caution by referee. Player's number noted by referee in his book.

BOOTS. Soccer shoes.

BOXING. Goalkeeper punches ball with fist away from goal.

BREAKAWAY. Player with ball has cleared defender and threatens goal in a one on one situation with the goalkeeper.

CONCACAF. Countries that belong to same soccer district as U.S.: Canada, Mexico, Central America, and the Caribbean Islands.

CAUTION. Referee signals warning with yellow card to player guilty of unnecessary roughness or ungentlemanly conduct.

CENTER. Long kick from side of field to center; same as cross.

CENTER CIRCLE. Circle, 10-yard radius, in center of field where kickoffs are placed at start of game, second half, and after goal.

CHARGING. Legal use of body to lean on opponent when he is in playing distance of ball. Cannot be violent.

CHIPPING. Pass made by lofting ball with back spin that causes ball to grip turf and not roll far.

CLEARING. Long kick to get ball out of defensive end.

CORNER ARC. Pie-shaped wedge, one yard in radius, in each corner of field. Ball must be placed within for corner kick.

CORNER KICK. Direct free kick from corner mark awarded to attacking team when defensive team last plays ball over its own goal line.

CORNER MARK. Flags at corner of field to help linesmen determine whether ball is over touchline or goal line.

COVER. Back-up support of defense. If attacker beats defender, another defender steps up to cover for him.

CROSS. Ball kicked from one side of field to middle or to other side of field.

CUP PLAY. Tournament competition.

DANGEROUS PLAY. Actions dangerous to opposing player; results in indirect free kick.

DEAD BALL. Ball not in play.

DEFENDER. Player who is given responsibilities of stopping opposing attacker.

DELAY. Defensive tactic to slow attack in middle section of field long enough for defense to regroup.

DEPTH. A condition in which a defender is backed up by other defenders. A defense where players cover for each other has depth.

DIAGONAL RUN. Movement crossfield.

DIP SHOT. Ball that starts out high, then plunges like knuckleball; difficult for goalie to save.

DIRECT FREE KICK. Awarded for serious foul such as pushing, holding, kicking, striking, handling ball, charging in dangerous manner, and tripping. Ball can be knocked directly into goal by the kicker.

DISTRIBUTION. Giving out passes.

DRAW. 1. A tie.

2. To pull an opponent to you in order to get by him, or open a space for a teammate or the ball.

DRIBBLE. Moving the ball with rapid touches of the foot without passing or shooting.

DROP BALL. Means of putting ball into play after suspension of play when possession is in doubt. For example, 2 players from opposing teams kick ball out of bounds simultaneously. Referee drops ball to the ground between 2 players to restart play.

DUAL SPEARHEADS. Twin center forwards.

DUMMY. Running toward the ball as if to play it, but letting it go by for a fellow player to pick up.

ECONOMICAL TRAINING. Multi-purpose drills that emphasize fitness, technique, and tactics altogether.

EXTRA TIME. Allotted by referee for injuries, or when ball flies great distance out of play, or for other suspensions of playing time.

FIFA. Fédération Internationale de Football Association. World governing body of football; headquarters in Zurich, Switzerland.

FAR POST. Goal post furthest from ball.

FEINT. Deceptive movement by player to draw an opponent off balance.

FIRST TOUCH. Play ball by passing or shooting without settling it first.

FLAT. Two defenders positioned side by side so that they cannot provide backup support for each other.

FOOTBALL. Refers either to game of soccer or the ball itself.

FORWARD. Player who usually leads attack on opponent's goal.

FRONT RUNNER. Player who has run behind defense with ball and is racing for shot on goal. A breakaway.

FUNCTIONAL TRAINING. Drills that allow players to practice the responsibilities of their individual positions.

FUNNEL DEFENSE. Tactic where backs and midfielders withdraw part way into their own defensive sector without engaging the attacking opponents.

GOAL. 1. A score.

2. The uprights and crossbar whose inside dimensions are 24 feet wide by 8 feet high.

GOAL BOX. Six-yard area directly in front of goal.

GOALIE. Goalkeeper responsible for keeping ball out of goal; only player who can use hands, as long as he is inside penalty area.

GOALKEEPER. Same as above.

GOAL KICK. When ball goes over end line off attacking team, results in indirect free kick for defensive team; ball must be kicked from 6-yard box on side ball went out.

GOAL LINE. Line that extends from one corner flag to another. Endline.

GOAL MOUTH. Area right in front of goal.

GOALPOSTS. Uprights.

HALFBACK. Plays in middle of field; links attack and defense. Midfielder.

HALF-TIME. Ten-minute interval between 2 45-minute halves.

HALF VOLLEY. Shot or pass off incoming ball kicked as ball hops or bounces.

HALFWAY LINE. Line connects touch lines at center of field, divides field in half.

HANDBALL. Ball touched intentionally by arms or hands; results in direct free kick.

HEAVY GROUND. Muddy, wet field.

HOLDING. Obstructing opponent's movement with your hands or arms.

INDIRECT FREE KICK. Awarded for lesser violations, such as obstructing opponent, ungentlemanly conduct, illegal substitution, illegal charge, dangerous play, goalkeeper carrying ball more than 4 steps in penalty area without losing possession, and offsides; ball must be touched by 2 players before it can enter goal.

INJURY TIME. Extension of play due to time for injury during regular play.

INSWINGER. Ball kicked from side and curved in toward goal.

INTERVAL TRAINING. Alternating vigorous exercises with short intervals of rest.

JUNIOR PLAYER. Player, registered with U.S. Soccer Federation, who has not reached nineteenth birthday.

JUGGLING. Using different body parts to rebound ball in air successively without letting it touch ground.

KEEPER. Goalie.

KICKOFF. Start of play at beginning of game, or at halftime, or after goal; ball is not in play until it first rolls forward 26 inches, or one circumference.

KILLER PASS. Pass made to player running between 2 defenders in such a way it ends up behind defense for scoring attempt.

LAWS. Rules of game; there are 17 altogether.

LEAD. To pass ball ahead of receiver.

LIBERO. Player who is mainly responsible for defense but has free rein to attack when he can.

LINESMEN. Stand on side of field with flag to signal offsides, out of bounds, and assist referee in calling fouls.

LOB. High soft kick over heads of opponents. Same as chip shot.

MARKING. Covering man to prevent him from receiving ball or advancing.

MATCH. A game.

MATURE GOAL ATTACKS. Those that penetrate inside line of defense and result in shot at goal.

MIDFIELDER. Halfback.

MOLDED SHOES. Rubber cleated shoes worn on hard grass fields.

NASL. North American Soccer League; largest in U.S. (1967).

NSCAA. National Soccer Coaches Association of America; organization of soccer coaches throughout U.S.

NEARPOST. Post closest to ball.

OBSTRUCTION. Player blocks another from ball when neither is in playing distance of ball; results in indirect free kick.

OFFSIDE. If attacker does not have two defenders between him and goal, (one is usually goalkeeper), he is offsides unless he is: (1) not involved in play; (2) in own half of field; (3) in corner kick situation; (4) in drop ball situation; (5) in instance of goal kick; (6) when ball is last played by defense; (7) when he is in possession of ball; (8) when ball is ahead of him; or (9) on a throw-in.

OFFSIDE TRAP. Tactical maneuver to catch attacking player offside; entire defense steps up when ball is to be played behind it, therefore, placing attacker in offside position.

OFF THE BALL. Running without the ball either to distract opponent or into vacant space to receive pass.

ONE TOUCH. Shooting or passing at first contact with the ball.

ONE-TWO. Give and go without stopping incoming ball, same as wall pass.

ORDERED OFF. Player expelled from game.

OUTSWINGER. Ball that veers out away from goal.

OVERLAP. An attacking play where a player overtakes another player from behind and advances into a more dangerous position. Normally a midfielder or defender will overlap a forward to confuse the defense.

PACE. Speed at which game is being played.

PENALTY AREA. 18-yard by 44-yard rectangle in front of goal in which goalkeeper may use his hands; direct kick infraction inside this area results in penalty kick.

PENALTY KICK. Direct free kick given as result of personal foul within penalty area; taken by 1 player from spot 12 yards in front of goal; only the goaltender may defend.

PENALTY SPOT. Mark on field 12 yards in front of goal.

PENETRATION. Attacking deep into defense to set up scoring chance.

PITCH. Field of play.

POST. Uprights of goal.

PRESSURE DEFENSE. Low pressure: easy defense executed in middle and attacking thirds of field; chief tactic is to fall back and delay, but become highly concentrated in final third. High pressure: constant chasing of ball wherever it is, tight marking.

PROFESSIONAL. Player reimbursed with money.

PUNCHING. Boxing the ball out; goalkeeper tactic.

PUNT. A long kick by goalkeeper holding ball in his hands.

PUSH PASS. Inside of foot pass.

RED CARD. Card shown by referee to player for violent flagrant fouls. Follows yellow warning card and means player must leave field of play immediately.

REFEREE. Single man in charge of entire game: timekeeping, scoring, judging of fouls.

RESTART. When ball is out of bounds, or ball is dead, game must be restarted by corner kick, goal kick, kickoff, indirect or direct free kick, or drop ball.

RHYTHM. Tempo of game.

RUN. A sprint from one to another position to receive ball or to make space for someone else.

SAVE. Goalkeeper stops ball from entering goal.

SCREEN. To retain possession of ball and protect it by placing your body between it and the opponent, same as shielding.

SETTLING. Trapping the ball.

SHOT. A kicked or headed ball toward the goal in an attempt to score.

SIDELINE. Line on each side of field marking out-of-bounds. Same as touchline.

SLIDE TACKLING. Player hurls himself along the ground with one leg extended to block ball from opponent.

SPEARHEAD. Center forward who attacks goal as far upfield as possible.

SQUARE PASS. Pass made at right angle towards sideline.

STEALING. Taking the ball from an opponent without physical contact.

STRIKER. Forward whose main purpose is to score goals.

STUDS. Type of shoes worn on wet, soft turf; has longer cleats than molded rubber-soled shoes; provides better traction.

SUPPORT. Defensive or attacking player who comes to help teammates.

SWEEPER. Player behind defense who collects all through balls and supports side of defense ball is on.

SWERVES. Shot on goal that curve right or left for deception.

SWITCH. Two players intentionally change positions.

SYSTEM. Physical formation of players on field; for example, 4–2–4; 4–3–3.

TACKLING. Attempting to take a ball by force from an opponent.

TACTICS. Methods of play.

TARGET PLAYER. Forward whom team looks to right away when it gains possession of ball. Main job is to pass the ball to other forwards.

TEAM MANAGER. English name for coach.

TECHNIQUE. Skills for game.

THROUGH PASS. Pass that goes directly up the field, usually to beat the last line of defense for a shot. Same as killer pass.

THROWER. Player throwing in the ball from out of bounds.

THROW-IN. Action used to get ball back in play after out-of-bounds over touchline.

TOUCH. Ability to feel and controll ball.

TOUCHLINE. Sideline between the 2 corner flags.

TRAPPING. Settling of air or ground ball so it comes to rest at feet.

TWO TOUCH. Touching incoming ball only twice, the first to stop it, the second to get rid of it.

USSF. United States Soccer Foundation; governing body in U.S. soccer.

UPFIELD. Attacking sector.

VOLLEY. To kick an incoming ball before it hits the ground.

WALL. Defensive maneuver in which group of players form a blockade to help the goalie prevent a score on direct or indirect free kicks; must be a minimum of 10 yards from the ball.

WALL PASS. Player A passes to teammate who makes a first-time pass behind defender for player A to collect; same as give and go.

WARNING. Yellow card, a caution.

WIDTH. Spacing players across the field, touchline to touchline, to cover all zones, rather than bunching them toward the center.

WING. An area of the field near the touchline.

WINGER. Player who stays on outside and attacks from flanks.

WORLD CUP. World championship held every 4 years, sponsored by FIFA; 16 teams are in finals. Each country selects team and enters worldwide regional competition 2 years in advance.

YELLOW CARD. Caution card. First warning. Next violation means expulsion from game.

Laws of the Game

Throughout the world, boys, girls, men, and women all play soccer under one set of rules. These rules are called *Laws of the Game;* and have evolved over 100 years. In the United States, our high school and college officials have rewritten many of the laws to meet their needs; however, it will only be a matter of time until all soccer in the United States conforms to the *Laws of the Game* as prescribed by FIFA. Therefore, the synopsis below is of FIFA laws and not high school federation or collegiate rules.

Law I. Field of Play

(The size of the goal and field should be reduced for younger children.)

	Maximum	*Minimum*
Length	130 yds.	100 yds.
Width	100 yds.	50 yds.

Recommended: Length 120 yds.
Width 75 yds.
Goal: 8 ft. x 24 ft.

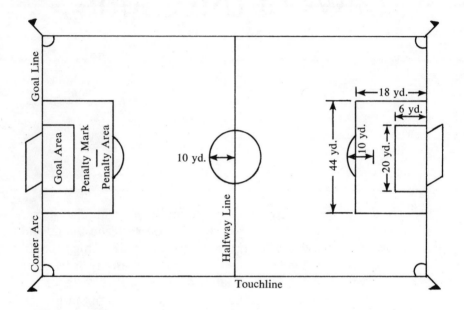

Law II. The Ball

The ball shall be spherical and have a circumference of not more than 28 inches and not less than 27 inches. The weight of the ball shall not be more than 16 ounces nor less than 14 ounces. A smaller, lighter ball may be used for younger children.

Law III. Number of Players

A game shall be played by two teams of eleven players each. One player on each team shall be designated as the goalkeeper.

Substitutes: International games provide for only two substitutes; however, the number that can be used is up to the national association. In the United States this decision is left to the individual leagues. When a team substitutes for its goalkeeper, the referee must be notified as to who the new goalkeeper is. No player who has left the game in favor of a substitute, may re-enter the game.

Law IV. Players' Equipment

1. A player shall not wear anything that is dangerous to another player.

2. Footwear need not be worn, but shoes must conform to the following standards:
a) Studded—studs shall not stick out of the shoe more than ½ inch nor have a rounded radius of less than ¼ inch
b) Molded—legal

3. The uniforms:
a) Goalkeeper shall wear colors that distinguish him from all other players on the field
b) Field players shall wear jerseys of contrasting colors to distinguish the teams. They must wear jerseys, shorts, and stockings.

Law V. Referees

The referee's powers granted to him by the *Laws of the Game* commence when he enters the field of play; he is responsible for the following:

1. Enforcing the Laws

2. Not penalizing when an advantage is gained by the attacking team

3. Keeping a record of the game
a) Time
b) Goals
c) Substitutions

4. Using discretionary power to stop or suspend play

5. Using discretionary power to caution a player for not playing within the laws

6. Allowing no person to enter the field other than the 22 players and 2 linesmen

7. Stopping the game if a player has been seriously injured

8. Sending off a player, any player, who in his opinion is guilty of violent conduct or use of abusive language

9. Restarting play after suspended play

10. Deciding on all equipment, the ball, the field, and the goals

Law VI. Linesmen

Two linesmen shall be appointed to:

1. Indicate when the ball is out of play and indicate:
a) Corner kick
b) Goal kick
c) Throw-in

2. Assist the referee in controlling the game in accordance with the laws. Some instances would be:
a) Fouls
b) Goals
c) Offside

Law VII. Duration of the Game

The duration shall be two equal periods of 45 minutes (shorter for younger children).

1. Allowance shall be made in either period for all time lost through accident or injury, the amount of which shall be determined at the discretion of the referee.

2. Time shall be extended to permit a penalty kick to be taken.

The half-time interval shall not exceed 5 minutes except by consent of the referee.

Law VIII. The Start of Play

1. At the beginning of the game:
a) Team winning the toss of the coin shall have its choice of kick-off and end of the field it will defend.
b) Every player must be in his own half, and the defending team must be 10 yards from the ball.
c) The ball is in play when it has traveled its own circumference forward. The kicker shall not play the ball a second time until another player has played the ball.

2. After a goal is scored the game shall be restarted as at the beginning of the game, by the team losing the goal.

3. At half-time, ends shall be changed, and the kickoff shall be taken by the team which did not open the game.

4. After any temporary suspension:
a) If the ball leaves the field of play, the game is restarted as it would have been if there were no suspension.
b) If the ball does not leave the field of play, the game is restarted by a drop ball. The referee drops the ball between two players of opposing teams. The ball must strike the ground before it can be played. If these rules are not complied with, the drop ball shall be retaken.

Law IX. Ball In and Out of Play

The ball is out of play:

1. When it is entirely over the goal line or touch line. It does not matter whether it is on the ground or in the air.

2. When the referee stops play.

3. If the ball rebounds off of goals, corner flag, referee, or linesman (if he is on the field of play) the ball is in play.

Law X. Method of Scoring

A goal is scored when the ball passes entirely over the goal line, under the crossbar, and inside the uprights. It shall not be a goal if it is carried, thrown, or batted intentionally with the hand or arm. The team scoring the most goals is declared the winner.

Law XI. Offside

An attacking player is offside if he is nearer his opponent's goal line at the moment the ball is played unless:

1. He is in his own half of the field.

2. There are two opposing players between the goal and the attacker.

3. The ball was last played by a defender.

4. It is a throw-in.

5. It is a goal kick.

6. It is a corner kick.

7. It is a drop ball.

8. He is not involved in the play.

Law XII. Fouls and Misconduct

The following 9 offenses shall result in a direct free kick:

1. Kicking or attempting to kick an opponent

2. Tripping

3. Jumping at an opponent

4. Charging violently at an opponent

5. Charging from behind unless opponent is obstructing

6. Striking or attempting to strike an opponent

7. Holding an opponent

8. Pushing an opponent

9. Handling the ball (except goalkeeper in the penalty area)

If a defender intentionally commits one of the offenses in the penalty area, the attacking team shall be awarded a penalty kick.
The following 5 offenses shall result in an indirect free kick:

1. Dangerous play

2. Charging at an improper time

3. Obstructing an opposing player from the ball, without playing the ball

4. Charging the goalkeeper

5. Goalkeeper taking more than four steps while in possession of the ball

A player shall be sent off the field if he:

1. Is guilty of violent conduct

2. Uses abusive language

3. Persistently conducts himself in an ungentlemanly way after receiving a caution

An indirect kick shall be awarded if a breach of the laws has not already been committed.

Law XIII. Free Kick

Direct free kick: A free kick on which a goal can be scored directly. Indirect free kick: A free kick on which a goal cannot be scored until the ball is touched by another player.

The following considerations should be taken into account:

1. The ball shall be stationary.

2. The kicker is only allowed to touch the ball once, and it must roll over its full circumference.

3. All defending players must be 10 yards from the ball or on their own goal line.

4. Any free kick taken within the penalty area must clear the penalty area on the first play. Otherwise the kick is to be retaken.

Law XIV. Penalty Kick

The penalty kick is awarded when one of the fouls for a direct free kick occurs in the penalty area of the defending team.

Defensively:

1. All defenders must be taken out of the penalty area and remain at least 10 yards from the ball until kick is taken.

2. The goalkeeper must stand (without moving his feet) on the goal line between the goalposts until the kick is taken.

Offensively:

1. All attacking players, except the one taking the kick, must be out of the penalty area and 10 yards from the ball until kick is taken.

2. The person taking the kick must take the kick in a gentlemanly way. He may only contact the ball once.

Law XV. Throw-In

A throw-in results when the ball travels entirely over the touchline; the throw-in will be taken at the point where the ball went out of bounds. The following things should be kept in mind:

1. The ball must be thrown equally with two hands.

2. The thrower must face the field of play.

3. The ball must be thrown from in back of the head in one continuous motion.

4. Both feet must remain on the ground and in back of the touchline until the ball is released.

5. The ball is in play as soon as it enters the field of play; the thrower cannot touch the ball until it has been touched by another player.

On an improper throw-in, the ball is awarded to the opposing team.

Law XVI. Goal Kick

A goal kick is awarded the defending team when the ball passes over the goal line, outside of the goalposts, if last played by the attacking team. The kick shall be taken from the side where the ball went out and within the goal area. The ball must be played out of the penalty area by the goalkeeper on the first play. All defending players must remain out of the penalty area until the ball leaves the penalty area. The goal kick is retaken if these rules are not followed.

Law XVII. Corner Kick

A corner kick is awarded when the ball passes over the goal line outside the goalposts, last being played by the defending team. The ball shall be placed entirely inside the corner arc on the side the ball went out. The direct kick is taken, and all defending players must be 10 yards from the ball. The ball can only be kicked once by the player taking the corner kick.

Bibliography

Bradley, Gordon and Toye, Clive. *Playing Soccer the Professional Way.* New York: Harper and Row, 1973. Instruction book with good pictures of form and technique.

Csanádi, Arpád. *Soccer.* New Rochelle: Sportshelf, 1972. Two volumes. First-rate in-depth study of all aspects of game.

DiClemente, Frank F. *Soccer Illustrated.* New York: A. S. Barnes, 1955. Excellent illustrations of basic techniques.

Fédération Internationale de Football Association (FIFA). *Laws of the Game and Universal Guide for Referees,* English edition. Zurich: FIFA. The official word on how to play the game.

Glanville, Brian. *Soccer.* New York: Crown, 1969. Top journalist's instructive and highly entertaining account of the game.

Hughes, Charles F. *Tactics and Teamwork.* Yorkshire: EP Publishing, 1973. Hughes is manager of England Amateur Team.

Kane, Basil G. *Soccer for American Spectators.* New York: A.S. Barnes, 1970. Who's who in American pro soccer, etc.

Miller, Al. *Winning Soccer.* Chicago: Henry Regnery, 1975. Good section on conditioning exercises.

Vannier, Maryhelen and Poindexter, Hally Beth. *Physical Activities for College Women.* Philadelphia: W. B. Saunders, Co., 1969. Chapter 24, pp. 405–421, deals with soccer.

Vogelsinger, Hubert. *How to Star in Soccer.* New York: Four Winds Press, 1967. Compact guide.

Wade, Allen. *Soccer: Guide to Training and Coaching.* New York: Funk and Wagnalls, 1967. Excellent analysis of modern tactical development.

Other noteworthy books

Batty, Eric. *Soccer Coaching the Modern Way.* London: Faber, 1969.

Domini, Enzo. *The Book of Soccer.* New York: Van Nostrand Reinhold, 1972.

Humiston, Dorothy and Michel, Dorothy. *Fundamentals of Sports for Girls and Women: Team and Individual.* New York: Ronald Press, 1965.

Liss, Howard. *Soccer.* New York: Funk & Wagnells, 1968 (paperback edition, New York: Hawthorn Books, 1975).

Smits, Ted. *The Game of Soccer.* Englewood Cliffs, N.J.: Prentice-Hall, 1968.

Woosman, Phil. *Sports Illustrated Soccer.* Philadelphia: Lippincott, 1972.

Magazines

Soccer America, a weekly. Clayton G. Berling, P.O. Box 9393, Berkeley, Calif. 94709.

Soccer Journal, a quarterly. National Soccer Coaches Association of America. Don Y. Yonker, editor, 949 Welling Road, Elkins Park, Philadelphia, Pa. 19117.

Soccer Monthly. United States Soccer Foundation, Inc., 350 Fifth Avenue, New York, N.Y. 10001.

Soccer World, a bi-monthly. World Publications, Box 366, Mountain View, Calif. 94040.

Films

The following films are available from the United States Soccer Football Association Film Library, 350 Fifth Avenue, New York, N.Y. 10001.

		Rental Charge
Fair or Unfair Tackling (Law XII), 16mm, black & White, 20 minutes		$ 5.00 per wk
Football Technique by FIFA Coach Dettmar Cramer		$50.00 per wk
Reel 1	"Ball Gymnastics" "Ball Lifting" "Dribbling"	
Reel 2	"Ball Control" "Passing" "Shooting"	Reels can be rented separately for $12.50 each.
Reel 3	"Heading" "Goalkeeping" "Throw-in"	
Reel 4	"Pendulum Training"	
Four Step Rule for Goalkeepers, 16mm, color, sound, 10 minutes		$ 5.00 per wk
The Name of the Game is Football, 16mm, color, sound, 15 minutes		$ 7.50 per wk
Skills of Football, 16mm, color, sound, 30 minutes		$10.00 per wk
Towards Uniformity of Interpretation (Law XII), 16mm, color, 40 minutes		$10.00 per wk

Index